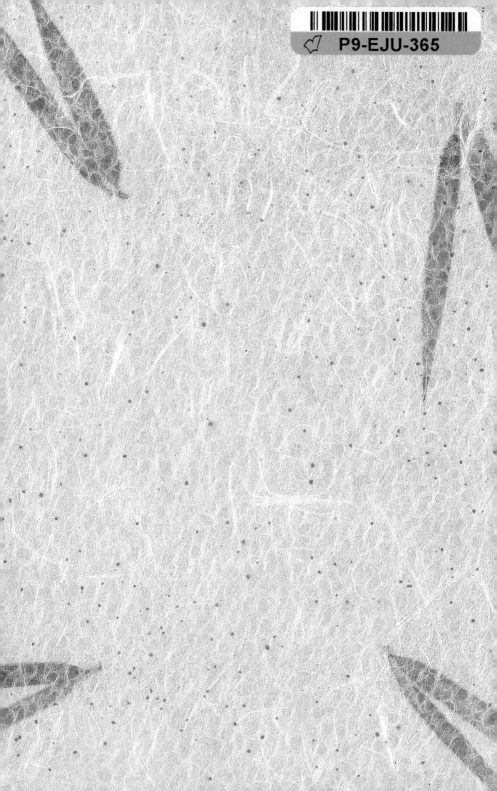

PERFECT
DIGESTION

DEEPAK CHOPRA, M.D.

PERFECT

DIGESTION

the key to

balanced living

Harmony Books / New York

Published by Harmony Books, a division of Crown Publishers, Inc., 201 East 50th Street, New York, New York 10022. Member of the Crown Publishing Group.

Random House, Inc. New York, Toronto, London, Sydney, Auckland

Harmony and colophon are trademarks of Crown Publishers, Inc.

Manufactured in the U.S.A.

Design by Lauren Dong

Library of Congress Cataloging-in-Publication Data

Chopra, Deepak.
    Perfect digestion : the key to balanced living / by Deepak Chopra, M.D.
    Includes bibliographical references and index.
    1. Irritable colon—Alternative treatment. 2. Digestive organs—Diseases—Alternative treatment. 3. Medicine, Ayurvedic.
4. Digestion. I. Title.
RC862.I77C48 1995
616.3'4—dc20   95-30583

ISBN 0-517-79975-8

10 9 8 7 6 5 4 3 2 1

First Edition

CONTENTS

INTRODUCTION

As a physician, one supremely important truth has been brought home to me again and again: That the human body is a crowning achievement of nature, a gift bestowed upon each of us to appreciate and to care for throughout our lives. But enjoyment of this gift requires a certain degree of understanding—an informed awareness of our bodies' needs that is more crucial today than ever before.

Let me explain why this informed awareness is so important now. Among the many accomplishments of American civilization, none is more impressive than the fact that virtually no one in the United States is starving to death, which was not true in centuries past and is hardly the case even today in many parts of the world. Throughout much of history, human beings had little choice but to eat whatever they could find, hunt, or grow. This had many drawbacks, but it did cause the evolution of our remarkably flexible human digestive system, which is not only capable of processing a wide variety of foods but is actually best suited to doing so.

After tens of thousands of years, the parameters of human nutrition changed quite suddenly. At least in the United States, most
of us no longer have to eat whatever we can get. On the contrary, we may eat whatever we want—but what we seem most
often to choose is an ever-narrowing range of foods that are
mostly sweet, or high in fat content, or low in dietary fibers. Our
digestive system, which evolved to deal with scarcity and variety, is now called upon to handle abundance and nutritional uni-
formity. In other words, although we have enough to eat today,
we're not really taking advantage of the foods available to us.
We're eating too much of the wrong things, and we're often doing it in such a rush that more stress than nutrition is delivered
to our bodies and our cells. While Western society has largely
solved the problems of making food available, we have yet to
learn how to make the choices that are best for us. In terms of
learning about the foods we eat and understanding how our bodies process them, we have yet to recognize our true needs.

Although the larger purpose of this book is to bring you a
more enlightened interpretation and a more comprehensive understanding of your physiology as a whole, our explicit focus
here is on the gastrointestinal tract. It certainly deserves our attention. According to Ayurveda, the traditional Indian science
of health, most diseases originate as an imbalance in the digestive system. In the pages ahead we look at how the gastrointestinal tract is constructed, how it works when healthy, and
how to restore health when ideal functioning has been lost
through imbalance or disease.

Our discussion of the gastrointestinal (GI) tract will be concerned especially with the tract's lower end, which includes the
intestines and the colon. Naturally, these are not topics that
most people take up in casual conversation. Yet even as far back
as the time of the ancient Greeks, when the philosopher
Epicurus declared that sound digestion was the basis of all human goodness, people have recognized the importance of the
gastrointestinal tract. It's interesting that Epicurus, who cele-

brated the pleasures of good digestion (and whose name brought us the term *epicurean*), also believed that poor digestion was so morally destructive that everything possible should be done to avoid it. He himself eventually converted to a diet of water and grain in order to minimize the risk of stomachache.

When functioning as it should, your GI tract converts food into energy and nutrition to build, repair, and sustain your body—a big job that continues every minute of every day throughout your lifetime. Over seventy years an average American's digestive system will process about twenty-three thousand pounds—nearly twelve tons—of solid food. When you're in a state of good health, food passes through the twenty-seven feet of digestive canals linking throat to rectum without any conscious effort on your part and without any significant discomfort. Yet comfort is by no means common to everyone. Studies show that as many as one in every three Americans experiences frequent and significant discomfort related to the lower intestinal tract. Indeed, during the course of any given day almost everyone has gastrointestinal symptoms of some kind, and studies indicate that at least 20 million Americans suffer from a well-defined constellation of symptoms known as Irritable Bowel Syndrome, or IBS.

IBS has had other names throughout the years: spastic colon, nervous stomach, mucous colitis, irritable colon, and many more. Although it is commonly referred to as "chronic colitis," this is actually incorrect since the word *colitis* implies inflammation of the bowel, which does not exist in true IBS. The fact that Irritable Bowel Syndrome has so many names suggests that it is not really a disease at all, but a collection of signs and symptoms that have become commonplace in modern medicine. So commonplace, in fact, that more people present themselves in the offices of gastroenterologists—specialists in the GI tract—with symptoms of IBS than with any other complaint.

In this book we will consider in detail such manifestations of IBS as constipation, diarrhea, and gas. Although not generally life-threatening, these can cause a great deal of discomfort, in-convenience, worry, and even great emotional turmoil. We will also look briefly at some of the more serious problems that can afflict the gastrointestinal tract. Severe conditions such as ul-cerative colitis, Crohn's disease, and diverticulitis are beyond our primary focus here, but familiarity with their early symp-toms is vital in order to deal with them effectively.

PERFECT
DIGESTION

THE QUANTUM MECHANICS

OF DIGESTION

From a holistic point of view, understanding any aspect of the human body—whether it's digestion and elimination or the way we process sights and sounds—must begin with a view of the body as a single integrated system in which all the parts are designed to function in a unified manner.

Although the gastrointestinal tract is itself a fascinating and marvelously complex apparatus, it is still only one aspect of the intricate and often bewildering entity that is our physical self. For this reason, I believe it's appropriate to begin by offering you a new understanding of your body as a whole—one could even say a new vision of it. I believe that once you've viewed yourself from this new perspective, you will see yourself as you did before, but with an important foundation on which to build a program of truly perfect health—that is, a healthy GI tract and a healthy body overall.

The new perspective is derived from Ayurveda, so in a sense it's not really a new perspective at all, because Ayurveda is the oldest health care system known to man. Remarkably, this ancient approach to understanding the body, which has been tested and proven over thousands of years, is also completely compatible with our contemporary understanding of how nature works. In fact, Ayurveda simply uses a different terminology to express some of the most advanced ideas of molecular biology and quantum physics.

The first principle of this new/old perspective is that the human body is not a solid, particulate, static, fragmented, "frozen sculpture" that exists in isolation from the rest of nature. Rather, Ayurveda recognizes the body as part of the natural continuum. From this point of view, the human body is a dynamic field of energy. It is constantly participating in an exchange with the larger of field of energy that surrounds it, which comprises the rest of the universe. Most remarkably of all, as a result of his continual exchange, your body is being renewed and replaced every moment of your life!

If you could see your body as it really is at the most basic level, you would realize that 98 percent of the atoms in your anatomy were not there a year ago. For example, scientific research has shown that your bones—which seem so solid and which support your entire frame—are re-created brand new every three months. This means that while the configuration of the bone cells remains constant, the billions of atoms that comprise the bones and pass freely back and forth through the cell walls are constantly undergoing change and replacement. As a result, you acquire a new skeleton every three months.

The same processes are at work throughout the rest of your body. The cells in your liver turn over very slowly, but new atoms still flow through them, like water in a stream, creating a new liver every six weeks. Your skin is new every month. Even within the brain—where cells do not regenerate when they die—the specific atoms of carbon, hydrogen, nitrogen, and oxygen are totally different today from what they were one year ago. In the digestive tract, you construct a new stomach lining every four days, and the surface cells that actually come in contact with digesting food are renewed every five minutes. Basically, your body completely re-creates itself down to the last atom over a period of four or five years.

It is as if you live in a building whose bricks are constantly being taken out and replaced. From one day to the next it looks like the same building, but in fact it's fundamentally different. A human body also looks much the same from day to day, but it is forever in a process of change and exchange with the universe around it. And this process includes the basic physiological functions of metabolism, digestion, and elimination.

All the renewing and re-creating I've mentioned is very carefully controlled. It must be, in order to rebuild the body in recognizable form rather than as a haphazard collection of parts. Where does this careful control originate? In a word, it originates with intelligence.

This brings us to the first and perhaps the most important Ayurvedic principle: Our physiology itself is inherently intelligent, and the many physiological functions guiding the replacement of cells and molecules and even atoms are dependent on the inherent intelligence that inhabits the human body.

In recent years, quantum physics has provided us with these same basic insights into the nature of human functioning. The body is made up of atoms. And what are atoms? It may be easiest to think of them as particles whirling at lightning speed through vast empty spaces—colliding, disintegrating, darting back and forth—but atoms are not really particles in the sense that a pebble is a particle of rock or a twig is a piece of tree. Rather, they are minute fluctuations of energy in the infinite expanse of energy that modern physics calls the *unified field*. It is from the unified field that all natural forces emerge, giving rise to an entire material universe, including your body.

Fundamentally, your body is as void of matter as is intergalactic space. It may be surprising to realize that an apparently solid mass of living, breathing matter is in reality mostly empty space—nothing more than a perceptual illusion, a reflection of the more basic underlying intelligence that structures the entire universe. It may indeed be surprising, but nature's truth often is.

This perspective on human physiology, which recognizes intelligence as the basic fabric from which the body is structured, gives rise to the concept of the *quantum mechanical body*. This phrase pays homage to another crucial principle: that the body's inner intelligence is the ultimate and supreme genius that mirrors the intelligence of the universe as a whole.

These lofty notions may seem somewhat removed from the explicit focus of this book. In order to bridge that gap, let us first try to locate the mechanisms of the body that are responsible for healing—or, as I prefer to express it, for re-creating health. Obviously, no single organ is responsible; every part of the body is able to recognize when it is damaged and is capable of initiating healing. This in itself is an astonishing miracle, and as yet we have no simple answers to explain how it is even possible. Every one of the thousands of processes involved in healing even a superficial wound is incredibly complex and incompletely understood. Although countless articles have been written about the clotting process of blood, for example, it remains true that no medical intervention can reproduce the healing action that takes place in a tiny cut on your finger.

According to Ayurveda, the ability to heal is the primary and most significant quality of the body. Ayurveda defines healing as a process of returning the body to its natural functions. This is accomplished by enlivening the intelligence inherent in every cell of the body. When Hippocrates declared thousands of years ago that only nature itself can bring about healing, he was expressing a truth that is still valid today, despite all our technological advances.

Consider, for example, the case of a broken arm. A skilled physician will align the bone fragments in such a way as to minimize the effort nature needs to effect healing. The wise doctor creates conditions that help to support the restoration of health, but he or she always recognizes that something beyond the physician's power performs the actual work of healing.

Digestion plays a critical role in the natural healing process. The constant renewal of every part of the physiology is dependent on proper digestive functioning, which Ayurveda sees as a means of extracting intelligence from food and then processing it to support the intelligence inherent in the entire physiology. In this way, the process of digestion plays a pivotal role in maintaining overall homeostasis and healing power. It is through digestion that intelligence, in the form of nutrients from the body's surrounding environment, is extracted, broken down, and then combined again in such a way as to re-create every cell, every organ, every tissue of the human body.

Let me emphasize this point. To many people, it may seem strange to find digestion discussed in terms of intelligence. After all, in the West we're used to associating intelligence with the brain, not with the stomach or the intestines. But Ayurveda recognizes the intelligence that exists in every organ, in every cell, of the body.

All the functions of your body have inherent balance points, which are set by the natural intelligence we've been discussing. This is really quite remarkable: The millions of molecules in your bloodstream, for example, travel where they're needed with unerring accuracy; the pupils of your eyes are always adjusting to changing light conditions with greater flexibility than any camera lens you could ever hope to buy; your body temperature is constantly falling or rising as your internal thermostat reacts to the temperature of the air, to the time of day, and to your level of exertion. And all the while, your digestive system is moving along with the efficiency of an assembly line in a well-run factory.

It is only when this balance is disrupted for some reason, when the set points of your physiology are disturbed, that symptoms begin to occur. When that happens, your task is not so much to defeat or suppress the symptoms as it is to restore balance to your system, whereupon the symptoms will disappear by themselves.

For digestion and metabolism to perform with their natural precision and efficiency, a well-balanced lifestyle is the first prerequisite. Unhealthful food, poor sleeping habits, negative emotions, or physical and mental strain all can cause the body to deviate from natural functioning. Perhaps it is the central role that digestion plays in the constant restoration of the body's intelligence that makes it so exquisitely sensitive to all of the influences that comprise modern life. It may be for this reason that "gut" problems are among the most common complaints in contemporary health care.

From an Ayurveda perspective, then, there are no well-defined edges to our bodies—no borders, no boundaries. The study of digestion is inseparable from an understanding of the neurological and cardiovascular systems, just as the human body itself is inseparable from its environment.

The body is part of the larger unified field, and our being extends beyond the confines of this bag of skin and bones to the far reaches of the cosmos. Our thoughts, imaginations, feelings, desires, and energies are as much "us" as are our fingernails, our blemishes, and our digestive tracts. Why should we give more regard to physiological artifacts? Why should we think that any imperfection in them is more a part of us than is our infinite awareness, which is capable of reaching the stars in the blink of an eye? In fact, we are the stars. We are the rivers, we are the storms, we are the floods, we are the galaxies. These are all projections of our awareness.

But to fully experience this awareness, we need our physiology. Seeing, hearing, feeling, smelling, digesting—we need all of these in order to sense and understand the universe we live in. Therefore, our intention in this book is to re-create healthy balance not only in every cell of the intestinal tract but in every aspect of the quantum mechanical body.

Now you're ready to take some practical actions toward fulfilling that intention. You should begin by keeping a record of any gastrointestinal symptoms you have during the day, together with your feelings before and during the occurrence of the symptoms. This will help reveal any patterns to your symptoms and any relationships that exist between them and fatigue, stress, and other emotional factors.

At the end of this chapter, you'll find several IBS Tracking Sheets on which to record your symptoms. Keep a copy of this form with you throughout the day, and use it anytime you undergo discomfort in the intestinal tract.

One point that will quickly become evident is that the triggers for your symptoms may be accumulating over a period of days or even an entire week rather than coming on suddenly within hours or minutes. Events that took place days ago may be causing the discomfort you're experiencing right now. While a given food or beverage may produce diarrhea and cramping within a few hours, feelings such as stress or anger can have a more long-term effect. You may find that several stressful days or sleepless nights cause your symptoms "suddenly" to get much worse. But after reviewing your tracking sheets, you'll discover that the pattern was actually quite clear.

Perhaps the most important function of this record keeping is to document your improvement as you begin implementing the recommendations in this book. For this reason, in addition to using your tracking sheets each time you have a symptom I would like you to make a record each time you have a bowel movement, noting whether it is normal or abnormal in its nature. Over time, as you observe improvement, you will be tracking your own growth toward perfect health.

IBS TRACKING CHART

The following chart can help you understand the characteristics and causes of IBS symptoms you may be experiencing. This understanding is an important first step toward making changes that will eliminate the problems. If you notice, for instance, that your symptoms always occur after a large evening meal, you may want to begin eating less substantial dinners. And simply making yourself aware of your symptoms in an organized way can have powerful therapeutic benefits.

The chart, however, should not be used as a tool for self-diagnosis or as a substitute for medical evaluation of health concerns. If your symptoms persist, see your doctor. Do so immediately if you experience rectal bleeding or unusual weight loss.

Use the IBS Tracking Chart for at least four weeks. If it's convenient, photocopy the chart and continue to use it for a more extended period. With the insights you'll gain into the specific nature of your IBS complaints, you'll be able to use the information in this book much more effectively.

A brief explanation of the chart's categories:

Type of Symptom	Did you experience diarrhea, constipation, cramping, gas, or some other IBS complaint?
Severity	Rate your degree of discomfort on a 1–10 scale. If you're consistently experiencing the same symptom, does it seem to be getting better or worse over time? What variables may be affecting this?
Duration	Did the symptom come on suddenly and then disappear, or did it persist for a period of time?
Last Meal	What did you eat or drink prior to symptom's onset? How long ago?
Stress Level	How were you feeling emotionally when the IBS symptom appeared? If you were under stress—at work, for example—what was the cause? (As you continue to use the chart over a period of days, look for patterns in this category that suggest changes you can initiate.)
Comments	At the end of each week, write down pertinent observations. What factors seemed to affect your digestion? Consider influences that may have taken place before the actual appearance of symptoms, since stress does not always manifest itself immediately. Think about how you can alter specific behaviors to benefit your digestion. If you make changes, note any effects on the following week's chart.

WEEK ONE						
	Time of Day	Type of Symptom	Severity (1–10)	Duration	Last Meal	Stress Level
Mon.						
Tues.						
Wed.						
Thurs.						
Fri.						
Sat.						
Sun.						

Comments:

WEEK TWO						
	Time of Day	Type of Symptom	Severity (1–10)	Duration	Last Meal	Stress Level
Mon.						
Tues.						
Wed.						
Thurs.						
Fri.						
Sat.						
Sun.						

Comments:

WEEK THREE					
Time of Day	Type of Symptom	Severity (1–10)	Duration	Last Meal	Stress Level
Mon.					
Tues.					
Wed.					
Thurs.					
Fri.					
Sat.					
Sun.					

Comments:

WEEK FOUR					
Time of Day	Type of Symptom	Severity (1–10)	Duration	Last Meal	Stress Level
Mon.					
Tues.					
Wed.					
Thurs.					
Fri.					
Sat.					
Sun.					

Comments:

2

DIGESTION AND THE

AYURVEDIC DOSHAS

In chapter 1 we saw how Ayurveda provides a unique foundation on which to build an understanding of the human body—a foundation that makes intelligence the basis of the entire physiology. Ayurveda breaks down the notion of a rigid separation between mind and body, and the wisdom of this should be obvious, for clearly any mental or emotional event gives rise to a corresponding event in the body. Ayurveda even has its own vocabulary for defining these mind/body conjunctions, and for describing the quantum mechanical principles that control the relationships between consciousness and physiology.

Ayurveda describes these principles in terms of three important governing agents called "doshas." These are ultimate, irreducible metabolic principles that regulate the flow of intelligence throughout the physiology. The names of the three doshas are Vata, Pitta, and Kapha. Each dosha has its own function in the body: Vata dosha controls all movement, Pitta is responsible for metabolism and digestion, and Kapha governs the structure of the body.

Every cell in your body must contain all three doshas in order to sustain life. Your body must have Vata—or motion—in order to breathe, to circulate the blood, pass food through the digestive tract, and send nerve impulses to and from the brain. It needs Pitta—or metabolism—to process food, air, and water through the entire system and to facilitate proper intellectual functioning. It requires Kapha—or structure—to hold cells together and to form muscles, fat, bones, and sinew.

In Ayurveda, the whole process of digestion is described through metaphors of heat and fire. When we say that Pitta is primarily responsible for digestion, we are referring to Pitta's control over *agni,* the digestive fire, and over the other metabolic processes necessary for the absorption of nutrients throughout the gastrointestinal tract. But the physical movement of food through the digestive tract is governed by Vata dosha, while the digestive fluids are governed by Kapha. Proper balance of all three—Vata, Pitta, and Kapha—is essential for ideal digestion and elimination.

Your psychophysiological individuality is defined by the amount or proportion of each dosha that you naturally contain. If we say that someone is a Vata type, we mean that the Vata qualities are more evident in that individual. Similarly, if we say that someone is a Pitta type or a Kapha type, it means that the Pitta or Kapha dosha is more dominant in that individual's nature. Basically, everyone has all three doshas, but we have them in combinations that are unique to each of us.

Knowing your body type will help you understand more about who you are and why you are experiencing any gastrointestinal symptoms. Below is the Body-Type Questionnaire, which will allow you to identify your dominant dosha. You should take a few minutes to complete it before reading any further.

AYURVEDA BODY-TYPE QUESTIONNAIRE

The following quiz is divided into three sections. For the first 20 questions, which apply to Vata dosha, read each statement and mark, from 0 to 6, whether it applies to you.

> 0 = Doesn't apply to me
> 3 = Applies to me somewhat (or some of the time)
> 6 = Applies to me mostly (or nearly all of the time)

At the end of the section, write down your total Vata score. For example, if you mark a 6 for the first question, a 3 for the second, and a 2 for the third, your total up to that point would be 6 + 3 + 2 = 11. Total the entire section in this way, and you will arrive at your final Vata score. Proceed to the 20 questions for Pitta and those for Kapha.

When you are finished, you will have three separate scores. Comparing these will determine your body type.

For fairly objective physical traits, your choice will usually be obvious. For mental traits and behavior, which are more subjective, you should answer according to how you have felt and acted most of your life, or at least for the past few years.

SECTION 1: VATA

	Does not apply		Applies sometimes			Applies most times	
1. I perform activities very quickly.	0	1	2	3	4	5	6
2. I am not good at memorizing things and then remembering them later.	0	1	2	3	4	5	6
3. I am enthusiastic and vivacious by nature.	0	1	2	3	4	5	6
4. I have a thin physique—I don't gain weight very easily.	0	1	2	3	4	5	6
5. I have always learned new things very quickly.	0	1	2	3	4	5	6
6. My characteristic gait while walking is light and quick.	0	1	2	3	4	5	6
7. I tend to have difficulty making decisions.	0	1	2	3	4	5	6
8. I tend to develop gas and become constipated easily.	0	1	2	3	4	5	6
9. I tend to have cold hands and feet.	0	1	2	3	4	5	6

	Does not apply		Applies sometimes			Applies most times	
10. I become anxious or worried frequently.	0	1	2	3	4	5	6
11. I don't tolerate cold weather as well as most people do.	0	1	2	3	4	5	6
12. I speak quickly and my friends think that I'm talkative.	0	1	2	3	4	5	6
13. My moods change easily and I am somewhat emotional by nature.	0	1	2	3	4	5	6
14. I often have difficulty falling asleep or having a sound night's sleep.	0	1	2	3	4	5	6
15. My skin tends to be very dry, especially in winter.	0	1	2	3	4	5	6
16. My mind is very active, sometimes restless, but also very imaginative.	0	1	2	3	4	5	6
17. My movements are quick and active; my energy tends to come in bursts.	0	1	2	3	4	5	6
18. I am easily excitable.	0	1	2	3	4	5	6
19. I tend to be irregular in my eating and sleeping habits.	0	1	2	3	4	5	6
20. I learn quickly, but I also forget quickly.	0	1	2	3	4	5	6

VATA SCORE

SECTION 2: PITTA

	Does not apply		Applies sometimes			Applies most times	
1. I consider myself to be very efficient.	0	1	2	3	4	5	6
2. In my activities, I tend to be extremely precise and orderly.	0	1	2	3	4	5	6
3. I am strong-minded and have a somewhat forceful manner.	0	1	2	3	4	5	6
4. I feel uncomfortable or become easily fatigued in hot weather—more so than other people.	0	1	2	3	4	5	6
5. I tend to perspire easily.	0	1	2	3	4	5	6

	Does not apply		Applies sometimes			Applies most times	
6. Even though I might not always show it, I become irritable or angry quite easily.	0	1	2	3	4	5	6
7. If I skip a meal or a meal is delayed, I become uncomfortable.	0	1	2	3	4	5	6
8. One or more of the following characteristics describes my hair: • early graying or balding • thin, fine, straight • blond, red, or sandy-colored	0	1	2	3	4	5	6
9. I have a strong appetite; if I want to, I can eat quite a large quantity.	0	1	2	3	4	5	6
10. Many people consider me stubborn.	0	1	2	3	4	5	6
11. I am very regular in my bowel habits—it would be more common for me to have loose stools than to be constipated.	0	1	2	3	4	5	6
12. I become impatient very easily.	0	1	2	3	4	5	6
13. I tend to be a perfectionist about details.	0	1	2	3	4	5	6
14. I get angry quite easily, but then I quickly forget about it.	0	1	2	3	4	5	6
15. I am very fond of cold foods, such as ice cream, and also ice-cold drinks.	0	1	2	3	4	5	6
16. I am more likely to feel that a room is too hot than too cold.	0	1	2	3	4	5	6
17. I don't tolerate foods that are very hot and spicy.	0	1	2	3	4	5	6
18. I am not as tolerant of disagreement as I should be.	0	1	2	3	4	5	6
19. I enjoy challenges, and when I want something I am very determined in my efforts to get it.	0	1	2	3	4	5	6
20. I tend to be quite critical of others and also of myself.	0	1	2	3	4	5	6

PITTA SCORE

SECTION 3: KAPHA

	Does not apply		Applies sometimes			Applies most times	
1. My natural tendency is to do things in a slow and relaxed fashion.	0	1	2	3	4	5	6
2. I gain weight more easily than most people and lose it more slowly.	0	1	2	3	4	5	6
3. I have a placid and calm disposition—I'm not easily ruffled.	0	1	2	3	4	5	6
4. I can skip meals easily without any significant discomfort.	0	1	2	3	4	5	6
5. I have a tendency toward excess mucus or phlegm, chronic congestion, asthma, or sinus problems.	0	1	2	3	4	5	6
6. I must get at least eight hours of sleep in order to be comfortable the next day.	0	1	2	3	4	5	6
7. I sleep very deeply.	0	1	2	3	4	5	6
8. I am calm by nature and not easily angered.	0	1	2	3	4	5	6
9. I don't learn as quickly as some people, but I have excellent retention and a long memory.	0	1	2	3	4	5	6
10. I have a tendency toward becoming plump—I store extra fat easily.	0	1	2	3	4	5	6
11. Weather that is cool and damp bothers me.	0	1	2	3	4	5	6
12. My hair is thick, dark, and wavy.	0	1	2	3	4	5	6
13. I have smooth, soft skin with a somewhat pale complexion.	0	1	2	3	4	5	6
14. I have a large, solid body build.	0	1	2	3	4	5	6
15. The following words describe me well: serene, sweet-natured, affectionate, and forgiving.	0	1	2	3	4	5	6
16. I have slow digestion, which makes me feel heavy after eating.	0	1	2	3	4	5	6
17. I have very good stamina and physical endurance as well as a steady level of energy.	0	1	2	3	4	5	6
18. I generally walk with a slow, measured gait.	0	1	2	3	4	5	6

	Does not apply		Applies sometimes			Applies most times
19. I have a tendency toward oversleeping, and grogginess upon awakening, and am generally slow to get going in the morning.	0	1	2	3	4	5 6
20. I am a slow eater and am slow and methodical in my actions.	0	1	2	3	4	5 6

KAPHA SCORE

FINAL SCORE

VATA   **PITTA**   **KAPHA**

HOW TO DETERMINE YOUR BODY TYPE

Now that you have added up your scores, you can determine your body type. Although there are only three doshas, remember that Ayurveda combines them in ten ways to arrive at ten different body types.

- **If one score is much higher than the others, you are probably a single-dosha type.**
    Single-Dosha Types
    Vata
    Pitta
    Kapha

You are definitely a single-dosha type if your highest score is twice as high as the next highest dosha score (for instance, Vata—90, Pitta—45, Kapha—35). In single-dosha types, the characteristics of Vata, Pitta, or Kapha predominate. Your next highest dosha may still show up in your natural tendencies, but it will be much less distinct.

- **If no single dosha dominates, you are a two-dosha type.**
    Two-Dosha Types
    Vata-Pitta or Pitta-Vata
    Pitta-Kapha or Kapha-Pitta
    Vata-Kapha or Kapha-Vata

If you are a two-dosha type, the traits of your two leading doshas will predominate. The higher one comes first in your body type, but both count.

   Most people are two-dosha types. A two-dosha type might have a score like this: Vata—80, Pitta—90, Kapha—20. If this was your score, you would consider yourself to be a Pitta-Vata type.

- **If your three scores are nearly equal, you may be a three-dosha type.**
    Three-Dosha Type
    Vata-Pitta-Kapha

However, this type is considered rarest of all. Check your answers again, or have a friend go over your responses with you. Also, you can read over the descriptions of Vata, Pitta, and Kapha on pages 19–22 to see if one or two doshas are more prominent in your makeup.

VATA

Characteristics of Vata Type

- Light, thin build
- Performs activity quickly
- Irregular hunger and digestion
- Light, interrupted sleep; tendency toward insomnia
- Enthusiasm, vivaciousness, imagination
- Excitability, changing moods
- Quick to grasp new information, also quick to forget
- Tendency to worry
- Tendency to be constipated
- Tires easily, tendency to overexert
- Mental and physical energy comes in bursts

It is very Vata to

- Be hungry at any time of the day or night
- Love excitement and constant change
- Go to sleep at different times every night, skip meals, and keep irregular habits in general
- Digest food well one day and poorly the next
- Display bursts of emotion that are short-lived and quickly forgotten
- Walk quickly

Change is the basic theme of the Vata personality. Vata people are unpredictable and much less stereotyped than either Pittas or Kaphas. Variability—in size, shape, mood, and action—is their main characteristic. For a Vata person, mental and physical energy appears suddenly. Vatas tend to walk quickly, to be hungry at any hour, to love excitement and change, to go to sleep at a different time every night, to skip meals, and to digest food well one day and poorly the next.

PITTA

Characteristics of Pitta Type

- Medium build
- Medium strength and endurance
- Sharp hunger and thirst, strong digestion
- Tendency to become angry or irritable under stress
- Fair or ruddy skin, often freckled
- Aversion to sun, hot weather
- Enterprising character, likes challenges
- Sharp intellect
- Precise, articulate speech
- Cannot skip meals
- Blond, light brown, or red hair (or reddish undertones)

It is very Pitta to

- Feel ravenous if dinner is half an hour late
- Live by your watch and resent having your time wasted
- Wake up at night feeling hot and thirsty
- Take command of a situation or feel that you should
- Learn from experience that others find you too demanding, sarcastic, or critical at times
- Have a determined stride when you walk

The theme of the Pitta type is intensity. Anyone with bright red hair and a florid face contains a good deal of Pitta, as does anyone who is ambitious, sharp-witted, outspoken, bold, argumentative, or jealous. The combative side of Pitta is a natural tendency, but it does not have to be blatantly expressed. When in balance, Pittas are warm and ardent in their emotions, loving, and content. A face glowing with happiness is very Pitta. It is also very Pitta to walk with a determined stride, to feel ravenously hungry if dinner is half an hour late, to wake up at night feeling thirsty, to live by the clock, and to resent having your time wasted.

KAPHA

Characteristics of Kapha Type

- Solid, powerful build; great physical strength and endurance
- Steady energy; slow and graceful in action
- Tranquil, relaxed personality; slow to anger
- Cool, smooth, thick, pale, and often oily skin
- Slow to grasp new information, but good retentive memory
- Heavy, prolonged sleep
- Tendency toward obesity
- Slow digestion, mild hunger
- Affectionate, tolerant, forgiving
- Tendency to be possessive, complacent

It is very Kapha to

- Mull things over for a long time before making a decision
- Wake up slowly, lie in bed a long time, and need coffee upon arising
- Be happy with the status quo and preserve it by conciliating others
- Respect other people's feelings (with which you feel genuine empathy)
- Seek emotional comfort from eating
- Have graceful movements, liquid eyes, and a gliding walk, even if overweight

Relaxed is the best word to describe the Kapha type. Kapha dosha, the structural principle in the body, brings stability and steadiness. It provides the physical strength and stamina that have been built in to the sturdy frames of typical Kapha people. Kaphas are considered fortunate in Ayurveda because as a rule they enjoy sound health. Moreover, their personalities express a serene and happy view of the world. It is very Kapha to mull things over for a long time before making a decision, to awaken slowly after lying in bed a long time, to seek emotional comfort from eating, to be happy with the status quo and to preserve it by conciliating others, and to genuinely empathize with other people's feelings.

While knowing your body type provides insight into your natural constitution and your physiological tendencies, you also need to consider whether the three doshas are balanced or unbalanced in your body. In general, Vata types are more likely to have Vata imbalances, Pitta types Pitta imbalances, and so on. However, this is not true in every case.

When an Ayurvedic doctor looks at any person, he or she sees signs of the three doshas everywhere. Although the doshas themselves cannot literally be seen, their effects can be recognized in all the physical characteristics of the body. And even though the doshas are invisible, they are tangible enough to be regulated, increased, decreased, and restored to balance.

When you watch a color television set, the screen appears to be filled with people, trees, animals, or buildings. But if you look more closely, it becomes clear that the images are made up of three kinds of dots, called "phosphors." The phosphors—which are red, green, and blue—are constantly shifting to form new images. Whether you see intact images or merely colored dots depends entirely on how close you are to the screen. Both perspectives are valid, but the dots are more fundamental because they are the raw material of the images. Therefore, if the picture goes bad, it is the phosphors that the repairman must adjust.

You can think of Vata, Pitta, and Kapha as three kinds of dots that comprise your entire body and every aspect of its functioning. The way your liver, kidneys, and heart work, your levels of insulin and other hormones, and the functioning of your digestive tract are all patterns formed by the shifting interplay of the three doshas. The role of the Ayurvedic physician is to adjust the body's functioning by returning the doshas to their natural state of balance. Any approach to a health problem depends on how the problem is perceived or understood, and even something as apparently "physical" as gastrointestinal complaints can be successfully approached through the doshas.

The Ayurvedic perspective is so comprehensive that it can account for all the possible combinations of symptoms to which different individuals may be subject. As a result, a physician trained in Ayurveda is able to individualize a patient's treatment program. The purpose of this book, however, is to offer recommendations that are simple and helpful to the greatest number of people. Recognizing and understanding your Ayurvedic body type is the first, all-important step toward recognizing which recommendations will be of the greatest benefit to you.

3

UNDERSTANDING YOUR

DIGESTIVE TRACT:

AN AYURVEDIC PERSPECTIVE

We have seen that the GI tract is one of the most important parts of the human physiology, yet it usually does its job virtually unnoticed, with very little conscious attention required. Although digestive processes are very complex, they are almost entirely automatic.

But what happens when things go wrong in the GI tract, and what are the factors most likely to cause disturbance? Of all of the things that can happen to the digestive tract, by far the most common is that constellation of symptoms discussed in chapter 1, collectively called Irritable Bowel Syndrome. In fact, IBS is sometimes referred to as the "common cold of the intestinal tract."

The first thing to realize about IBS is the tremendous variation in the symptoms that individuals can experience. Let's start with the most frequent indications.

• Abdominal pain, relieved by having a bowel movement. The pain is most commonly experienced in the lower left part of the abdomen, but its location and intensity may vary. Some individuals describe the pain as cramps, while others experience steady, dull, sharp, or even burning pain.

• A bloated or distended abdomen. This symptom also is commonly relieved by a bowel movement.

• Loose and frequent bowel movements along with abdominal pain. It is not uncommon for loose bowel movements to alternate with constipation.

• A feeling of incomplete evacuation. This is usually described as a sensation that, in spite of having had a bowel movement, you have not completely emptied your bowel.

While these are the most common symptoms, many others can occur as part of the IBS complex. Your symptoms, for example, may include chronic constipation without pain. Many individuals experience difficulty in passing stools, which may be small and hard or thin and "pencil-like." Or, like millions of people, your principal symptom may be too much gas, without any other serious complaints. Many people move from one symptom to another over a period of hours, days, or weeks. The important message of this chapter is that, from an Ayurvedic perspective, all IBS symptoms are related and can be understood as variations on a common theme.

Most people with IBS have at least two of the symptoms described above. A symptom that should not be present, however, is rectal bleeding. If you experience this symptom, you should immediately consult a physician. It is important for anyone having symptoms in the GI tract—or in any other part of the body—to receive professional care. I strongly urge you to consult your family physician for proper evaluation and diagnosis of your symptoms. The ideas in this book are intended as a supplement to Western medicine, not as a replacement.

In order to consider how symptoms arise in the GI tract, it is helpful first to have an overview of your digestive tract and the workings of its various parts. As I describe the different organs and their functions, you can refer to the drawing below.

THE DIGESTIVE SYSTEM

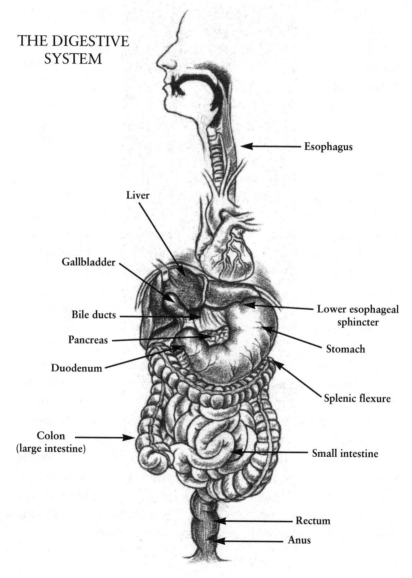

Esophagus

Liver

Gallbladder

Bile ducts

Pancreas

Duodenum

Lower esophageal sphincter

Stomach

Splenic flexure

Colon (large intestine)

Small intestine

Rectum

Anus

Let's begin our discussion of the digestive process where the process itself actually begins—in the mouth. As you chew a piece of food, digestive enzymes are secreted by the salivary glands located in your cheeks and under your tongue. Then, when you swallow, complex neuromuscular mechanisms ensure that the food enters your esophagus—the tube that takes the food to the stomach—rather than your trachea, which leads into the lungs. Although it's normally aided by the force of gravity, the muscular action of your esophagus is capable of transporting food to your stomach even if you're standing on your head (not a recommended posture for eating).

From the esophagus, food enters the stomach, where bacteria are killed by powerful acidic secretions and food storage takes place. Indeed, the small intestine, which follows the stomach in the GI tract, is largely a sterile environment as a result of the stomach's activities, although a number of parasites—such as tapeworms and hookworms—have the ability to pass through the stomach intact. Along with bacterial cleansing of swallowed food, digestion continues in the stomach by two means: mechanical grinding of the food takes place through the stomach's muscular action, while at the same time strong digestive enzymes are breaking the food down into its component parts.

It's interesting to note that although the hydrochloric acid and digestive enzymes in the stomach are powerful enough to attack and dissolve heavy proteins and meats, under normal conditions these acids do not harm the lining of the organ itself. When this natural protection is compromised, however, erosions of the stomach lining may result. These are known as peptic ulcers.

Ayurveda teaches that the digestive processes of both the mouth and the stomach are dominated by Kapha dosha. Kapha regulates liquids throughout the body, including saliva and the various secretions of the stomach lining. When the physiology of a Kapha individual is unbalanced, there may be nausea brought on by excessive production of stomach acids; an over-abundance of mucus may also be present, both in the GI tract and in the respiratory system. Attacks of vomiting are seen more frequently among Kapha types than in other individuals, as a result of mucus accumulating in the stomach. This can be brought on by overindulgence in Kapha-dominated foods, especially fatty meats and dairy products.

Upon leaving the stomach, food passes into the small intestine, which is in many respects the most important part of the entire digestive tract. This area is dominated by Pitta dosha, which controls the secretion of the small intestine's digestive enzymes.

The small intestine is not really small. It is narrow in diameter, but it's fully twenty feet in length. It is divided into sections, each of which has its own role in the digestive process. The interior is lined with millions of tiny projections called "villi," which, by greatly increasing the surface area, allow the intestine to absorb nutrients and to transport them into the bloodstream. Some of the most dangerous conditions that can afflict the small intestine involve an inability to absorb nutrition even though food may have been properly digested.

Michael Oppenheim, M.D., author of *The Complete Book of Better Digestion,* has pointed out that Western medicine tends to regard the small intestine as a remarkably disease-free organ. Although stomach cancer and especially colon cancer are common, malignancies of the small intestine rarely develop, and the small intestine is commonly exempt from the bleeding and irritation that frequently occur in other areas of the GI tract. In its wisdom, Nature seems to have given the small intestine a kind of special immunity, perhaps because it's the most vital of all the digestive organs.

From the Ayurvedic perspective, however, the small intestine can be the site of a great many disorders, particularly since it is the seat of agni, the digestive fire, which is discussed in detail in chapter 4. In Sanskrit, the small intestine is called *grahani*, meaning "that which grasps things." In other words, the small intestine, by process of absorption, "grasps" the essence of foods, and it is here that food is metabolized on the level of its nutritional intelligence.

Poor functioning of the small intestine can have many consequences, ranging from diarrhea, fatigue, and poor appetite to the more serious problem of malabsorption. Many Ayurvedic physicians view intestinal malabsorption as much more widespread than Western medicine acknowledges; since it is difficult to diagnose at low levels, it simply goes unrecognized by many people, as well as by their doctors, according to the Ayurvedic view.

An unhealthy diet is often the cause of intestinal malabsorption, particularly when one type of food is emphasized at the expense of all the others. In the United States, this usually means too many sweets or too much meat. But eating almost anything exclusively can damage the digestive fire. Ill-advised medications, such as laxatives and pain killers, or stimulants, such as caffeine, can also bring on this problem. Vata types, since they tend to drink a great deal of coffee, are especially prone to malabsorption.

The solution to intestinal malabsorption is a varied diet that avoids hard-to-digest foods or extremes of any kind. Meals should be of moderate size. Foods should be neither overcooked nor raw, and extremely hot or cold foods should be avoided. Buttermilk is very beneficial for this problem, as we'll see.

When the small intestine is functioning well, the nutritional intelligence it absorbs enters the circulatory system to nourish the entire physiology. Many nutrients travel to the liver, where intricate metabolic processes help convert the food into energy. The liver is also very active in removing toxic impurities from the system.

As a Pitta organ, the liver gives rise to such "hot" emotions as anger, envy, and ambition. As a result, Ayurveda teaches that the liver is prone to overheating, which is the cause of many inflammatory diseases.

Organs such as the pancreas and the gallbladder also assist in the complex job of digesting food. The pancreas plays an important role in digestion through the production of insulin and other hormones, while the gallbladder stores and secretes bile, an oily green liquid that is produced by the liver and assists in digestion of fats. All these functions are under the control of Pitta, which literally means "bile" in Sanskrit.

Normally, it takes three to five hours for food to pass through the small intestine, during which time many of the nutrients needed to support the body are absorbed. The remaining mixture of undigested food, mostly in liquid form, is now ready to pass into the colon, a muscular tube about four feet in length. The colon is also referred to as the "large intestine" because its diameter is approximately the size of your fist, whereas the small intestine has a diameter only about the size of your big toe. Within the colon, nutrients are absorbed that are vital to the brain and to the body's entire neurological system. This third and final stage of digestion is controlled by the Vata (air) dosha. Unbalanced Vata types are likely to suffer from gas or constipation owing to poor function of the colon.

From the esophagus to the beginning of the colon the gastrointestinal tract is almost free of bacteria. But the colon contains more than four hundred distinct bacterial species that play an active role in absorbing excess water and nutrients and in passing stools through the colon for eventual evacuation. In fact, about one-third of the material present in the colon is bacterial in nature, and it is estimated that up to half of the stool we pass each day is bacterial.

Depending on the individual, waste material may spend anywhere from four hours to three days moving through the colon before entering the last twelve inches of the digestive tract, which is the rectum. Once the material enters the rectum, it stretches the walls of the bowel and stimulates a reflex urge to have a bowel movement.

A person's pattern of elimination, as well as the physical characteristics of the stool itself, are key indicators of the quality of his or her digestion. It's important to pay attention to these very meaningful signs of physiological health or imbalance. If, for example, your stools have a consistently bad odor, this suggests the presence of toxins in your GI system as a whole, and particularly inadequate digestion in your large intestine. Ayurveda prescribes a number of spices for improving colonic absorption, the most common of which are black pepper, ginger, and nutmeg.

I hope this description conveys something of the wondrous complexity and precision of the digestive process as well as the relationships among its various parts. It is because of these integral relationships that a symptom related to the function of the colon—such as diarrhea, pain, or constipation, for example—may in fact have originated much farther up the digestive tract, or even outside the tract altogether. Other than the brain and the central nervous system, no other part of the human body is as sensitive to the numerous influences of environment and everyday living as is the digestive system.

4

How to Make Friends

with Your Gut

Since Ayurveda sees good digestion as one of the pillars of perfect health, it follows that poor digestion is a major factor in the production of disease. In fact, Ayurvedic medicine considers nothing to be more important to your overall health than the quality of your digestion. There is a saying in Ayurveda that if you had to choose between a proper diet along with poor digestion or a poor diet accompanied with ideal digestion, the latter choice would be the wiser. Of course, it's best to have both perfect digestion and proper diet, but the important point is that for a balanced diet to have its proper effect, digestion must be strong enough and balanced enough to properly assimilate the nutrients contained in that diet. Remember that every cell in your body has been created from the foods you've eaten. If the food has been used well, the cells will be built well. But if the food has been badly used, the process of disease has already started. Ayurvedic sages liked to say that if you could digest it properly, even poison could be good for you, while with poor digestion, a person can die from drinking nectar.

Because the process of digestion is described in Ayurveda as a heating process, one of the most important principles in Ayurvedic medicine is called *agni,* which translates as "digestive fire." Agni is nothing less than a divine power that exists within you and that governs the health of your physiology. When this internal fire is appropriately nourished and kept burning at proper intensity, all the systems of your body will flourish. Your GI system will digest food efficiently and distribute all the necessary nutrients to every cell, while at the same time burning off waste products without leaving deposits of toxins. Your whole body will be in tune. But neglect of the digestive flame can show up in any number of ways, from unpleasant breath and body odor to a weakened immune system and vulnerability to infection.

Ayurveda recognizes four distinct conditions of agni—too high, too low, too variable, or in perfect balance. To a great extent, these conditions are related to specific doshas. Pitta types, for example, tend to experience excessive appetite as a result of a digestive flame that burns too high. Kapha, the water dosha, can suffer from low agni, resulting in low energy levels and a tendency to put on weight even if food consumption is not excessive. Vata types, for whom change is characteristic in every area of life, are likely to undergo the extremes of hunger and loss of appetite that result from an excessively variable digestive flame. In general, agni can be strengthened and increased by most forms of exercise, or even by just breathing deeply for several minutes—an exercise that Ayurveda calls Pranayama. Agni is diminished by long periods of sleep, withdrawal from physical activity, and by large portions of heavy, oily, or sweet foods.

When you're hungry, the burning sensation you feel in your gut occurs because the agni is burning hotter. This burning should be understood as a signal that your body is ready to accept and process food. If you eat only at these times, your food will be properly digested. Many physiological problems are caused by eating at times when the digestive fires are not really calling out for fuel. Consequently, the food is converted into fat and toxins rather than energy. This is the basis for much of the overweight so common in the West.

When all of the body's systems are functioning in a normal and healthy way, the digestive tract produces as an ultimate result a substance known as *ojas*. Ojas is described in Ayurveda as a biochemical located at the meeting point between consciousness and physiology, like a bridge connecting intelligence and matter. Ojas serves to integrate the entire physiology at the point of mind/body junction.

Cherak, the ancient sage who was one of the first Ayurvedic physicians, described ojas this way: "It is ojas which maintains all living beings by its saturation, and without ojas no life of creatures exists. Ojas is the initial essence of embryo and also the essence of its nourishing material. It enters first into the cardiac cycle and if it is destroyed it leads to destruction. It is the sustainer of life in the heart, it is the cream of the nutrient fluids in the body."

Ayurveda teaches that when ojas is energetically produced by the body, there is a sense of overall lightness, excellent energy, strong appetite, balanced and comfortable digestion, regular elimination, strong immunity, superb physical strength, and great stamina. But perhaps the most important sign of the presence of ojas is a sense of emotional well-being and happiness. According to Ayurveda, ojas is literally the biochemical equivalent of bliss. This has enormously significant implications. By increasing the presence of ojas in your body, you can rebuild yourself into the physical manifestation of strength and good health.

There is another substance described in Ayurveda that is the opposite of ojas in every way. This chemical, *ama,* is of a sticky nature and has a marked tendency to obstruct the channels through which ojas normally flows.

Ama can result from improper dietary habits, a self-destructive lifestyle, imbalances in digestion, or many other factors. The most obvious difference between ojas and ama is that ojas makes you feel well, while ama makes you feel sick; in fact, ama is the precursor of most diseases. In addition, there are some specific signs of ama's presence in the body: a feeling of heaviness, weakness, or lethargy, increased susceptibility to infectious diseases, problems with digestion and elimination, fatigue, and fluctuations in appetite, energy levels, and emotional stability.

Many symptoms of Irritable Bowel Syndrome—constipation, for example—are caused by the production of ama. As ama accumulates, digestion becomes disturbed and more ama is produced in turn. If you have experienced IBS symptoms in your lower gastrointestinal tract, you very likely have experienced other ama-related symptoms as well, such as fatigue or frequent colds. There is also a very visible sign of ama that you may have noticed without recognizing its importance. This is a white coating on the tongue, which appears most often in the morning. This coating is quite literally ama, and when it is present on the tongue it is also present throughout the digestive canals of your body. And remember that Ayurveda recognizes these channels as existing not only as conduits for blood, lymph, and nutrients derived from food, but for the flow of life energy itself.

Elimination of ama from your physiology is an important first step in solving intestinal problems. There are two basic strategies for accomplishing this: First, you can strengthen your overall digestion, which will naturally retard the formation of further ama; second, you can begin to apply some gentle purification procedures in order to eliminate ama that may already have accumulated in your body.

Let's look at some Ayurvedic techniques for strengthening digestion. By mobilizing the body's own inner intelligence, these simple techniques can make digestion a comfortable and efficient process that will foster ojas and retard ama. Some of these procedures will require changes in your current habits, but I think you'll find that the benefits are immediately apparent.

Eat in a Settled and Quiet Atmosphere

This is one of the most important principles for the treatment of Irritable Bowel Syndrome and related complaints. In fact, it's one of the most important recommendations in this entire book. Few things contribute more to bowel irritability than such habits as eating on the run, eating while you're working, or engaging in arguments at mealtime. It is very important that you take your meals during a settled and pleasant time of day when you can be free of distractions. This is almost always possible, even if you're very busy and have only twenty or thirty minutes in which to eat.

You really must set everything else aside at mealtime in order to allow your body to focus only on eating and digesting. With your attention exclusively on the meal in front of you, you can savor all of the flavors and properly extract the intelligence from the food.

Take a Few Minutes to Rest Quietly After Your Meal

By relaxing at the completion of a meal, before returning to another activity, you can allow the digestive process to begin in an effortless way. But you may be in the habit of hurrying out the door just as you finish your last bite—or, worse, taking some of the food with you to eat on the run. Remember that another name for IBS is "nervous stomach," so resolve to be more calm and sensible about your eating habits.

While Ayurveda recommends that everyone spend a few minutes relaxing after a meal, I suggest that anyone with Irritable Bowel Syndrome should actually lie down for a few minutes after eating whenever possible. It's not necessary or desirable to go to sleep during this time, but lying on your back or on your left side for five to ten minutes allows the digestive process to begin more comfortably and naturally.

Many people also find it helpful to settle down for a few minutes before eating. Try sitting quietly by yourself for about five minutes before you begin your meal, and do so at the meal's conclusion, before returning to work or other activities. You'll find that this small investment of time can return major benefits to digestion and general health.

Always Sit Down to Eat

Sitting down relaxes the digestive tract, helps focus your awareness on the process of eating, and enhances enjoyment of your food. Even if you're just having a snack of a few grapes or raisins, take the time to sit down at a table.

Don't Eat When You're Upset

Most people with Irritable Bowel Syndrome have already discovered that eating when you're emotionally upset can trigger symptoms. If you're upset at mealtime, wait a few minutes or more until you're feeling calmer.

In his book *Gastrointestinal Health,* Steven Peiken, M.D., refers to some remarkably graphic demonstrations of the relationship between stress and satisfactory digestion. During the nineteenth century, an army surgeon was able to study a patient who, as a result of a gunshot wound, had developed a permanently open passage between the interior of his stomach and the surface of his body. Over the course of prolonged observation it became obvious that the patient's emotional state caused variations in the coating that protects the stomach lining, the "mucosa." When the patient was emotionally upset, there was also an increase in the production of acid and a slowing of normal stomach contractions, so that acid-rich secretions remained in the stomach longer than usual. Severe irritation resulted.

All this, of course, has been known to Ayurveda for thousands of years. As a Kapha organ, the stomach is fundamental to the structure and stability of the body in a physical sense; it is also closely tied to emotional equilibrium. In Ayurveda the stomach is sometimes referred to as the "mother" of the entire body.

Here is a technique that can help you settle down and minimize stress. Sit quietly and close your eyes for twenty or thirty seconds. With your eyes closed, you may become aware of uncomfortable physical sensations in your body that accompany your emotional distress, because every mental sensation has a corresponding physical effect. Just keep your eyes closed and simply allow yourself to experience the uncomfortable physical sensation for a few seconds. Don't try to resist it, just experience it. Within a minute or so, the sensation will usually weaken or even disappear. When you open your eyes, you may find that your emotional discomfort has also diminished. Once you're comfortable, proceed with your meal.

Avoid Overeating

Ayurveda says that we should eat to about three-fourths of our actual food capacity. Eating beyond this point doesn't leave enough room for the stomach to function properly, and ama is the result.

Three-fourths capacity is actually the point of maximum eating comfort, which gives a feeling of satisfaction without any sensation of having overeaten. It may take a bit of practice to end your meals at this point, especially if you're used to overeat-

ing, but in a short while you'll feel much more comfortable when you end your meals before you feel full.

Avoid Cold Foods and Iced Drinks

Cold foods and drinks tends to freeze the digestive fires and thereby make the production of ama more likely. In Ayurvedic terms, this problem may be described as a Vata imbalance, since Vata is cold and dry by nature. To remedy this, you should favor foods and drinks that are well cooked, warm, and soothing.

Many people find that it takes some effort to give up iced cold drinks, which may be a lifelong habit, particularly in warm weather. But within a few weeks most people no longer miss the cold drinks and actually feel better without them. An Ayurvedic herbal tea blend, called Vata tea, is an ideal substitute for the cold drinks you've been having. It's not only warm and soothing in its nature, but it's specifically formulated to help pacify Vata.

Don't Talk While Chewing Your Food

While chewing and swallowing, you should allow your senses to go inward and enjoy the taste, sight, and smell of the food. Not speaking while you have food in your mouth will help accomplish this. You can still have conversations at the dinner table, of course, but they should be of a settled and light nature. Mealtime is not an occasion for dealing with emotionally sensitive issues. For the same reason, business lunches should be avoided.

Eat at a Moderate Pace

By taking time to chew thoroughly, you'll enjoy your foo more, and you'll enhance the process of digestion. If you'r fast eater, I recommend a simple technique that, over time,

help you regulate your eating speed. After each bite of food has entered your mouth, simply put your fork or spoon down and don't pick it up again until that bite has been swallowed. After a week or two of doing this, you'll find that your pace of eating has naturally become more moderate.

Don't Eat Until the Preceding Meal Has Been Digested

Continuous snacking produces ama. Suppose you were cooking bean soup but you kept adding a new batch of beans every thirty minutes. The soup would never be completely cooked! When you snack throughout the day, your digestive tract is never able to properly process the food you've eaten.

How long should you wait between meals? For most people, complete digestion usually takes from three to six hours. If you feel like having a snack during that time, make it something light, like a piece of fruit or a warm beverage.

Favor Meals Made with Freshly Cooked Foods

Because fresh foods have the greatest intelligence value, they facilitate the production of ojas. Conversely, leftovers are harder to digest and are more likely to produce ama.

Although many people believe that raw foods are a good source of dietary fiber, Ayurveda points out that raw foods are harder to digest and are more likely to irritate the colon. While a certain amount of raw food, such as salad, is fine to include in your diet, cooked foods in general are easier to digest.

It may require a bit of effort to incorporate all these suggestions into your eating patterns. Lifelong habits may be difficult to amend even when you know that they're not beneficial to your health. But it's important to remember that these very patterns helped to create your digestive problems.

The checklist on pages 42–43 is based on the suggestions we've discussed. By making copies of the list and filling them out each day, you can change your eating habits in an organized and stress-free way. If you begin by incorporating just one suggestion, then add another each week, you can easily improve your daily eating routines.

Now that we've strengthened digestion, let's explore several strategies to purify the body, specifically designed to eliminate ama.

The first technique involves devoting one day each week to an entirely liquid diet. By liquefying all your food in a blender, you'll ensure that your meals are of a light consistency and are easily processed by the digestive tract. This strengthens digestion and at the same time eliminates ama from the system. Try following this liquefied diet once a week for one or two months, then decide whether you want to continue it. If you feel comfortable and notice obvious benefits, you can use the liquefied diet every week for an indefinite period, or you may want to cut back to just once a month. You'll probably find that it's easiest to follow this routine on days when you don't have many responsibilities, such as on the weekend.

Remember, this is not a fast. Anything can be included in your diet as long as it's liquefied. To liquefy a food, simply place it in a blender and add warm water. You may take the liquids or liquefied foods as often as you like during the day. Soups, herbal teas, fresh fruit or vegetable juices, and grains that have been blended with water are obviously very well suited to this routine, while meat, fish, and poultry are definitely much less so. Proceed according to your appetite. Some people will feel strong and energetic even while taking only fresh fruit juices all day. Others, who find that they need more substance in the diet, can liquefy grains and vegetables in order to feel more at ease.

BODY INTELLIGENCE TECHNIQUES CHECKLIST

Start using your checklist every time you eat, whether it is a full meal or a snack. This will help you monitor your progress in applying the techniques. If some of them seem too difficult, try the easy ones first. Then add a new technique every week until you have incorporated them all. For the first meal of the day, use the circles numbered with a 1 to check off the techniques you used. If you did not use a Body Intelligence Technique, leave the space blank. There are enough spaces to record four meals or snacks a day.

	Monday	Tuesday	Wednesday	Thursday	Friday	Saturday	Sunday
Ate in a settled and quiet atmosphere	1 ○ 2 ○ 3 ○ 4 ○	1 ○ 2 ○ 3 ○ 4 ○	1 ○ 2 ○ 3 ○ 4 ○	1 ○ 2 ○ 3 ○ 4 ○	1 ○ 2 ○ 3 ○ 4 ○	1 ○ 2 ○ 3 ○ 4 ○	1 ○ 2 ○ 3 ○ 4 ○
Ate at my regularly scheduled mealtime	1 ○ 2 ○ 3 ○ 4 ○	1 ○ 2 ○ 3 ○ 4 ○	1 ○ 2 ○ 3 ○ 4 ○	1 ○ 2 ○ 3 ○ 4 ○	1 ○ 2 ○ 3 ○ 4 ○	1 ○ 2 ○ 3 ○ 4 ○	1 ○ 2 ○ 3 ○ 4 ○
Sat down at a table to eat	1 ○ 2 ○ 3 ○ 4 ○	1 ○ 2 ○ 3 ○ 4 ○	1 ○ 2 ○ 3 ○ 4 ○	1 ○ 2 ○ 3 ○ 4 ○	1 ○ 2 ○ 3 ○ 4 ○	1 ○ 2 ○ 3 ○ 4 ○	1 ○ 2 ○ 3 ○ 4 ○
Didn't eat when upset	1 ○ 2 ○ 3 ○ 4 ○	1 ○ 2 ○ 3 ○ 4 ○	1 ○ 2 ○ 3 ○ 4 ○	1 ○ 2 ○ 3 ○ 4 ○	1 ○ 2 ○ 3 ○ 4 ○	1 ○ 2 ○ 3 ○ 4 ○	1 ○ 2 ○ 3 ○ 4 ○
Stopped eating when only 3/4 full	1 ○ 2 ○ 3 ○ 4 ○	1 ○ 2 ○ 3 ○ 4 ○	1 ○ 2 ○ 3 ○ 4 ○	1 ○ 2 ○ 3 ○ 4 ○	1 ○ 2 ○ 3 ○ 4 ○	1 ○ 2 ○ 3 ○ 4 ○	1 ○ 2 ○ 3 ○ 4 ○

Avoided cold foods and drinks	1○ 2○ 3○ 4○	1○ 2○ 3○ 4○	1○ 2○ 3○ 4○	1○ 2○ 3○ 4○	1○ 2○ 3○ 4○	1○ 2○ 3○ 4○
Didn't talk while chewing	1○ 2○ 3○ 4○	1○ 2○ 3○ 4○	1○ 2○ 3○ 4○	1○ 2○ 3○ 4○	1○ 2○ 3○ 4○	1○ 2○ 3○ 4○
Ate at a moderate pace	1○ 2○ 3○ 4○	1○ 2○ 3○ 4○	1○ 2○ 3○ 4○	1○ 2○ 3○ 4○	1○ 2○ 3○ 4○	1○ 2○ 3○ 4○
Ate only after the previous meal had been completely digested	1○ 2○ 3○ 4○	1○ 2○ 3○ 4○	1○ 2○ 3○ 4○	1○ 2○ 3○ 4○	1○ 2○ 3○ 4○	1○ 2○ 3○ 4○
Ate a freshly cooked and balanced meal	1○ 2○ 3○ 4○	1○ 2○ 3○ 4○	1○ 2○ 3○ 4○	1○ 2○ 3○ 4○	1○ 2○ 3○ 4○	1○ 2○ 3○ 4○
Sat quietly for a few minutes after eating	1○ 2○ 3○ 4○	1○ 2○ 3○ 4○	1○ 2○ 3○ 4○	1○ 2○ 3○ 4○	1○ 2○ 3○ 4○	1○ 2○ 3○ 4○

Always let comfort be your guide. When you use the liquefied diet properly, you should feel light and energetic throughout the day.

The second recommendation for eliminating ama from the system is a very special Ayurvedic purification technique. It sounds very simple, but you'll find that it has a powerful influence in purifying and strengthening the gastrointestinal tract.

All you have to do is sip hot water frequently throughout the day. As mentioned earlier, ama is sticky and greasy by nature. Hot water can dissolve ama from your system just as it dissolves grease from dirty dishes, and it can accomplish this gradually and comfortably. There is, however, a specific routine that you must follow in order to gain maximum benefit from this technique.

First, the water should be very hot—ideally, so hot that you've got to blow on it before you sip. But if you have difficulty drinking water this hot, adjust the temperature accordingly.

Second, be aware that the quantity of water you drink is less important than the frequency with which you drink it. For best results, the water should be sipped about every thirty minutes. If this seems too much for you, take at least one or two sips every hour.

You may have other liquids during the day as well—herbal tea, for example—but always take the hot water. And remember to do so as often as comfort allows—three or four times a day definitely is not enough. Perhaps the easiest way to accomplish this is to buy a good quality thermal container, fill it in the morning with boiling water, and use it throughout the day. In a short time you'll begin to appreciate the soothing and balancing effect of this technique. Once they've gotten used to it, most people even look forward to drinking the water on a frequent basis.

During the first few weeks you may urinate more frequently, and your urine may increase by even more than the amount you've increased your fluid intake. This is because the body is beginning to flush out ama and other impurities. It's a sign that something beneficial is happening to your system. Gradually, the frequency of urination should return to normal, but the ama will continue to be dissolved from the system.

In the West, we have grown accustomed to looking for chemical remedies for our health concerns. Many people expect or even demand that some form of medication be prescribed whenever they visit a doctor's office, regardless of what brought them there. This is not the Ayurvedic way. While recognizing that drugs can be of great benefit in many areas of health care, particularly in acute situations, Ayurveda teaches us to look elsewhere for solutions to chronic conditions that have developed from fundamental imbalances in the physiology. The herbal supplements that Ayurveda does recommend are not intended simply to alleviate symptoms; rather, their purpose is to strengthen the mind/body constitution at basic levels and to rectify the imbalances that underlie all symptoms. In any case, Ayurvedic herbs are not "drugs" in the sense that we've come to understand that word. Unlike the highly concentrated, mass-manufactured pills that comprise most of the prescriptions dispensed in pharmacies, herbs are simply derivatives of plants. Ultimately, they are manifestations of the sun's radiant energy, which has been transformed by the process of photosynthesis into a physical object. By taking the sun's energy into your body in herbal form, you are making contact with the source of all life. Be conscious of this profound connection whenever you take herbal supplements. Your high level of awareness will make the herbs even more effective.

Below are some Ayurvedic herbs that can benefit digestion. Although each person's needs are unique, combinations of these herbs have generally proved beneficial to digestive processes. They are available through Ayurvedic resources, whose addresses are provided at the back of this book.

- **Amalaki** relieves irritations throughout the gastrointestinal system and stabilizes the blood-sugar irregularities that underlie cravings for unhealthy foods.
- **Bibihitaki,** which has strong but safe laxative properties, is useful for expelling Kapha accumulations in the digestive organs.
- **Chitrak** reduces hyperacidity and ama accumulation. By facilitating absorption, it prevents stagnation in the GI system.
- **Dhanyaka,** known in the West as coriander, benefits Pitta conditions in the GI tract for which most spices and herbs are contraindicated.
- **Lavanga,** or cloves, have heating and energizing effects that stimulate digestion.

In this chapter we've covered a number of simple but effective techniques for strengthening digestion, for cleansing ama from the body, and, in short, for "making friends with your gut." In chapter 5, we'll look in detail at the foods and dietary regimens most helpful for the elimination of symptoms and for creating perfect health.

5

Diet and the Art of

Determining What to Eat

Without *proper diet medi-
cine is of no use, and with proper diet medicine is of no need.*

This is an old Ayurvedic precept, and it should come as no
surprise to anyone suffering digestive problems that diet is of
primary importance. It seems obvious that what we eat will
have a basic effect on how we digest and how we eliminate, yet
most doctors don't give sufficient attention to diet in the treatment of IBS and other bowel complaints. Perhaps one of the
reasons for this is the complexity of dealing with the many variations in individual responses to specific dietary measures. Yet,
from an Ayurvedic perspective, these variations are perfectly
understandable; how one responds to a given dietary instruction will depend to a great extent on which doshas have become unbalanced in the body.

The main distinction between modern Western nutrition and
the Ayurvedic perspectives can be expressed very simply. It is
the distinction between a strictly materialist view of reality and

a view that encompasses values at other levels as well. Western nutritionists believe that we can best understand our food by evaluating its material qualities. Think of the broad range of nutritional terminology that has become familiar to us all: protein, carbohydrates, fats, minerals, cholesterol, vitamins, calories, and many more. Each of these terms describes a particular material quality of the food; a calorie, for instance, is a unit of energy that a food produces when it's burned or metabolized by the body.

While there's no doubt that analyzing food according to its material qualities is a worthwhile method of evaluation, Ayurveda also considers a food's intelligence value. While recognizing the material value of food, Ayurveda also acknowledges that an even more basic influence exists in every substance. This influence, located at the point of mind/body junction, is what Ayurvedic intelligence really means.

Recognizing the central importance of intelligence is like recognizing that a tree is comprised of different structural elements such as branches, bark, leaves, and seeds. The most effective way to strengthen the tree is not by dealing individually with each part but by making a more basic approach through the sap, which carries nature's intelligence to each and every area of the tree. By calling our attention to this basic fact of a food's intelligence, Ayurveda simplifies the use of dietary measures in the treatment and prevention of disease, whether it's Irritable Bowel Syndrome or any other complaint.

Ayurveda provides a number of means for locating and identifying the qualities of intelligence in food. Perhaps the most interesting technique is based on the taste of the food itself.

When food speaks to your doshas it says many different things, but the primary information is contained in taste. As your taste buds greet a bite of food, an enormous amount of useful information is delivered to your body. By working with this information and following your instincts, you can eat a balanced diet easily and naturally.

Ayurveda recognizes six distinct tastes. Sweet, sour, salty, and bitter are the four with which you are probably familiar, but there are two others: pungent and astringent. All spicy, hot-tasting food is pungent, while astringent is a taste that has a drying quality and causes the mouth to pucker. Pomegranates and beans are both examples of the astringent taste.

Here are some further examples of each taste:

Sweet: sugar, honey, rice, pasta, milk, cream, butter
Sour: lemons, cheese, yogurt, plums, vinegar
Salty: any salty food
Pungent: chili peppers, cayenne, ginger, any hot spice
Bitter: greens such as endive, spinach, romaine lettuce
Astringent: beans, lentils, pomegranates, apples, pears

With the elegance that is characteristic of so many natural functions, the six tastes are digested in an orderly progression. Sweet is metabolized first, followed by sour, salty, pungent, bitter, and astringent. It is interesting to note, however, that this sequence does not parallel the order in which our foods are typically eaten. Sweets, in the form of desserts, are virtually always taken at the end of a meal, but it's really healthier—and better for weight control—if sweets are eaten first. Similarly, salads are easier to digest if they're taken last (which is quite common in Europe). It's important to look at a meal holistically. As we've discussed, the sequence of foods comprised in each meal is particularly important. Good digestion and good nutrition are more than a matter of simply knowing what to eat and in what quantity.

The six tastes play an important part in balancing a diet and in creating a feeling of satisfaction after eating. These tastes are exquisite indicators of the intelligence of our physiologies. We can detect sweet taste in a dilution of 1 in 200. Salt can be perceived in a dilution of 1 in 400; and bitter can be detected in a solution of 1 in 2 million. Nature has evolved and refined our sense of taste in order to allow food to speak to our doshas, and the dietary recommendations given in this chapter are derived from Ayurvedic knowledge of this exquisite sensitivity.

In the following pages we'll consider a number of dietary recommendations, some of which will be more useful depending on your particular symptoms. As you put the suggestions into practice, be sure to continue filling out the daily Body Intelligence Techniques Checklist provided in chapter 4 in order to determine what effect these changes are having on your digestion. Bear in mind that changes in your diet will exert their influence not just in the hours after the food is taken but over the next few days or even weeks.

The first recommendation is to try to include foods from all six tastes in your diet every day. A balanced diet will always have the six tastes present, but individual needs may require them in different proportions. For example, most people with IBS should avoid very hot spices such as curry, garlic, pepper, or mustard. Yet there is one pungent spice—ginger—that tastes hot but actually has a soothing effect on many IBS symptoms. A bit of ginger can be included during cooking, but a special blend of ginger, lemon juice, and salt can also be taken separately to stimulate digestion. To prepare this mixture, cut a thin slice from the end of a fresh ginger root, remove the peel, chop until very fine, and add a few drops of lemon juice and a pinch of salt. Ideally, the mixture should be eaten thirty minutes before lunch and dinner, but it can also be taken immediately before the meal to aid in digestion and soothe the large bowel.

For most people who experience IBS symptoms, spices such as turmeric, fenugreek, mint leaves, and coriander leaves will also be helpful. Mint has been used for thousands of years as a part of the treatment of IBS, and it's still a popular remedy in many parts of Europe in the form of peppermint oil capsules. Using fresh mint leaves is a very pleasant and effective way to utilize this herb, and the leaves can be incorporated into many foods or beverages. In addition, a special blend of spices and herbs is available that is soothing to both Vata and the digestive tract. This blend is called Vata churna ("churna" simply means powder). Vata churna can be sprinkled onto your food at the table or used in cooking. Vata churna will simplify your choice of spices, and most people enjoy its pleasant taste. It can be ordered from the Ayurvedic sources listed at the end of this book.

What foods should you avoid? Obviously, you should stay away from any food that has caused you frequent problems. But as you gradually strengthen your digestion, you may find that certain formerly difficult foods no longer affect you. Most people should avoid heavy dairy products such as milk, cream, ice cream, and butter, at least until their IBS symptoms are brought under control. However, many patients with IBS can benefit from ghee, or clarified butter. Taken in small amounts, you may find that ghee actually is soothing to your digestive tract. Information about purchasing ghee or preparing it at home is included at the end of the book.

Ayurveda also recommends avoiding cucumbers, green leafy vegetables such as spinach and kale, sprouts of any sort, and grapes. Deep fried, oily, or very greasy foods are difficult to digest and are also best avoided.

Since caffeine disturbs both Vata and Pitta, it's best to avoid coffee, tea, chocolate, and caffeine-containing soft beverages. Also, carbonated beverages of any sort irritate the digestive tract, as do alcohol and cigarettes.

In deciding which foods to include in your diet, the first important principle is: The fresher the food, the better. But remember that fresh does not necessarily mean raw. You should favor freshly cooked, balanced, wholesome meals, with plenty of freshly cooked vegetable and whole grains. As much as possible, avoid packaged foods and foods prepared with artificial chemicals and preservatives.

GRAINS

Rice, barley, corn, millet, buckwheat, and rye are all perfectly acceptable. These should be unsweetened, and if possible they should be organically grown.

HONEY

Honey is an ideal sweetener, although sugar can also be used in moderate quantities. It's worth mentioning that Ayurveda recommends never cooking with or heating honey, as this changes the structure of the honey and produces a toxic effect.

FRUITS

Fruits such as apples, pears, and oranges can be included in your diet, but one fruit that is often especially recommended for the treatment of IBS is the pomegranate. Pomegranates have an astringent taste, which for many people soothes the cramping and diarrhea associated with IBS.

LASSI

This traditional Ayurvedic beverage also has many benefits, and it is easily prepared from yogurt and water. Lassi has a very soothing and nourishing effect on the entire digestive tract and can be taken with lunch every day, as a snack in the late afternoon, or whenever you like. When made properly, most people also find it delicious. A specific lassi recipe for treating IBS is included at the end of this book.

FIBER

In recent years dietary fiber has become part of the treatment and prevention of many disorders, so it merits some detailed discussion.

Modern interest in dietary fiber began with the pioneering studies on indigenous African populations conducted by D. P. Burkett, M.D. He discovered that the typical African tribesman produced more than three times the quantity of stool per day than the typical Englishman. At the same time, he found that the incidence of appendicitis, colon cancer, diverticulosis, hiatal hernia, and other bowel problems was much lower in the African population. Dr. Burkett concluded that the reason for this was related to the large quantities of natural fiber in the diet of the African population. Conversely, more recent studies have linked low levels of dietary fiber to digestive complaints ranging from constipation to colon cancer.

Although fiber has become a buzzword for both the public and the medical profession, the average daily consumption of dietary fiber in the United States is still less than half that of many so-called underdeveloped nations, and it is also significantly less than the official recommendation of the National Cancer Institute.

Perhaps fiber consumption has remained low because of the focus on fiber supplements. While most physicians provide their patients with lists of high fiber foods, many people turn to supplements in order to avoid making basic changes in their eating habits. But since supplements have little or no taste and are unappealing as food, people generally do not stay with them for very long.

Ayurveda teaches that fiber and every other nutrient should come to us through the whole foods we eat, not through supplements. It simply isn't possible to acquire the full nutritional benefits of any substance once it has been removed from its natural context and turned into a pill or a powder.

MEAT

Years ago vegetarian diets were considered food fads, and adhering to them was thought to indicate a degree of mental imbalance. But today, of course, many nutritionists tell us that a well-balanced vegetarian diet is the best course for good health and longevity. Although Ayurveda has always recognized the benefits of a meatless diet, it's not necessary for you to become a vegetarian in order to gain the benefits of Ayurvedic techniques. In fact, since most Americans are committed to meat as a regular part of their diet, it's important to find a way to accommodate Ayurveda to this fact.

Ayurveda by no means recommends making sudden or dramatic changes in a diet that you may have been following for many years. Rather, changes should be made gradually and intelligently. Therefore, while you do not need to set a goal of becoming a vegetarian, I do recommend that you begin to increase the amount of fresh fruits, vegetables, and grains in your diet and that you diminish the amount of meat. You might try eating fewer meals containing red meats such as beef and pork, favoring chicken and fish instead. Then gradually adjust your diet so that one or two days each week are entirely vegetarian. In any case, always be sure that your meals are balanced, wholesome, and appealing. Many excellent vegetarian cookbooks are available that can help you achieve this.

The information above can be useful to anyone, but you can further individualize your choice of foods by giving consideration to your Ayurvedic body type.

If your primary symptom is constipation, for example, and you don't have any of the other symptoms associated with Irritable Bowel Syndrome, you may benefit from the Vata-balancing diet, which appears at the end of this chapter. Notice that the Vata-balancing diet encourages a number of relatively heavy foods; this is because Vata is light by nature. The Vata diet also allows all dairy products. It includes oils because the drying quality of Vata is a common cause of constipation.

If loose and frequent bowel movements are your primary symptoms, either with or without abdominal discomfort, you may find that following the Pitta-balancing diet is most useful for you. Or the Kapha diet may be indicated by your symptoms. If you're not sure which diet is best for you, follow the instruction provided in this chapter for one or two months. Then, if you're not satisfied with your progress, try switching to one of the specific dosha regimens as dictated by your symptoms and your body type.

There is one more important point to cover before we leave the area of diet, and that is how to eat your meals. Chapter 4 provided some recommendations for making mealtimes calmer, quieter, and more settled. But there is another technique that is very helpful in treating Irritable Bowel Syndrome, and it's related to what I said earlier about the order in which the six tastes are taken during a meal. This technique involves eating each meal in a specific sequence, and taking care to eat only one food at a time. There are two main reasons why this sequence diet can be useful for people with IBS. First, eating foods one at a time makes the work of digestion a little less difficult for your body. Second, by eating the foods in a particular sequence that mimics the order in which the body actually digests them, you can further minimize the amount of digestive work your body has to do to accomplish the task thoroughly. The sequence diet, then, is basically an ama-reducing diet, because ama is the residue of incomplete digestion.

Ayurveda relies on several factors to determine the optimum sequence of foods, but the most important point is that heavier foods should be eaten earlier in the meal and lighter foods toward the end.

A simply analogy should make this principle clear, and it's based on the fact that agni is described as a "digestive fire." Imagine that you are building a fire and that you've already put into it the quantity of wood that the fire can consume within a reasonable period of time. Then, suddenly, someone dumps a truckload of heavy lumber on top of the fire. The fire will most likely be smothered as a result. This dumping of a truckload of wood at the end is analogous to taking a heavy dessert at the end of a meal. When we eat until we are quite full and then proceed to add something that is sweet and difficult to digest for the final course, ama results.

For this reason, I want to point out benefits of taking dessert at the beginning of a meal rather than at the end. You may find, as many children do, that eating dessert first is actually a delightful experience. And if you still desire something sweet later, a piece of fruit can be taken at that time. Bear in mind that since lunch should be the main meal of the day, it's especially important to follow the sequence diet at lunchtime. Even if you actually consume more food than usual, you will most likely be able to follow this regimen with no discomfort at all in your GI tract.

VATA-BALANCING DIET

1. *Favor* foods that are warm, heavy, and oily.
   Minimize foods that are cold, dry, and light.
2. *Favor* foods that are sweet, sour, and salty.
   Minimize foods that are spicy, bitter, and astringent.
3. Eat larger quantities, but not more than you can digest easily.

SOME SPECIFIC RECOMMENDATIONS

- **Dairy.** All dairy products pacify Vata.
- **Sweeteners.** All sweeteners are good (in moderation) for pacifying Vata.
- **Oils.** All oils reduce Vata.
- **Grains.** Rice and wheat are very good. *Reduce* barley, corn, millet, buckwheat, rye, and oats.
- **Fruits.** Favor sweet, sour, or heavy fruits, such as oranges, bananas, avocados, grapes, cherries, peaches, melons, berries, plums, pineapples, mangoes, and papayas. *Reduce* dry or light fruits, such as apples, pears, pomegranates, cranberries, and dried fruits.
- **Vegetables.** Beets, cucumbers, carrots, asparagus, and sweet potatoes are good. They should be cooked, not raw. The following vegetables are acceptable in moderate quantities if they're cooked, especially with ghee or oil and Vata-reducing spices: peas, broccoli, cauliflower, celery, zucchini, and green, leafy vegetables. It's better to avoid sprouts and cabbage.
- **Spices.** Cardamom, cumin, ginger, cinnamon, salt, cloves, mustard seed, and small quantities of black pepper are good.
- **Nuts.** All nuts are good.
- **Beans.** *Reduce* all beans, *except* tofu and split mung-bean soup.
- **Meat and fish** (for nonvegetarians). Chicken, turkey, and seafoods are all right; beef should be avoided.

PITTA-BALANCING DIET

1. *Favor* foods that are cool and liquid.
   Minimize foods that are hot in temperature.
2. *Favor* tastes that are sweet, bitter, or astringent.
   Minimize spicy, salty, or sour tastes.

SOME SPECIFIC RECOMMENDATIONS

- **Dairy.** Milk, butter, and ghee are good for pacifying Pitta. *Reduce* yogurt, cheese, sour cream, and cultured buttermilk (as their sour tastes aggravate Pitta).
- **Sweeteners.** All sweeteners are good except honey and molasses.
- **Oils.** Olive, sunflower, and coconut oils are best. *Reduce* sesame, almond, and corn oil, all of which increase Pitta.
- **Grains.** Wheat, white rice, barley, and oats are good. *Reduce* corn, rye, millet, and brown rice.
- **Fruits.** Favor sweet fruits, such as grapes, cherries, melons, berries, avocados, coconuts, pomegranates, mangoes, and sweet, fully ripened oranges, pineapples, and plums. *Reduce* sour fruits, such as grapefruits, olives, papayas, persimmons, and sour, unripe oranges, pineapples, and plums.
- **Vegetables.** Favor asparagus, cucumbers, potatoes, sweet potatoes, pumpkins, broccoli, cauliflower, celery, okra, lettuce, beans, green beans, zucchini, and green leafy vegetables such as lettuce. *Reduce* hot peppers, tomatoes, carrots, beets, onions, garlic, radishes, spinach, and mustard greens.
- **Beans.** *Reduce* all beans, *except* tofu and split-mung dhal.
- **Spices.** Cinnamon, coriander, cardamom, and fennel are good. But the following spices strongly increase Pitta and should be eaten only in small amounts: ginger, cumin, black pepper, fenugreek, cloves, celery seed, salt, and mustard seed. Chili peppers and cayenne should be avoided.
- **Meat and fish** (for nonvegetarians). Chicken, pheasant, and turkey are preferable. Beef, seafood, and egg yolk increase Pitta and should be avoided.

KAPHA-BALANCING DIET

1. *Favor* foods that are light, dry, and warm.
   Minimize foods that are heavy, oily, and cold.
2. *Favor* foods that are spicy, bitter, and astringent.
   Minimize foods that are sweet, salty, and sour.

SOME SPECIFIC RECOMMENDATIONS

- **Dairy.** In general, *avoid* dairy products, *except* low-fat milk.
- **Fruit.** Lighter fruits, such as apples and pears, are best. *Reduce* heavy or sour fruits, such as oranges, bananas, pineapples, figs, dates, avocados, coconuts, and melons, since these fruits increase Kapha.
- **Sweeteners.** Honey is excellent for reducing Kapha. *Reduce* sugar products, as these increase Kapha.
- **Beans.** All beans are fine *except* tofu, which increases Kapha.
- **Nuts.** *Reduce* all nuts.
- **Grains.** Most grains are fine, especially barley and millet. *Avoid* wheat and rice, as they increase Kapha.
- **Vegetables.** All are fine, *except* tomatoes, cucumbers, sweet potatoes, and zucchini, as they increase Kapha.
- **Spices.** All spices are good except salt, which should be avoided, as it increases Kapha.
- **Meat and fish** (for nonvegetarians). White meat from chicken or turkey is fine, as is seafood. *Reduce* red meat.

6

THE ROLE OF YOUR

EMOTIONS

One of the most important factors in Irritable Bowel Syndrome is the relationship between your emotions and your gut. For most people with IBS, this relationship is very soon made clear both by their physicians and by their experiences in life. There simply is no doubt that mental turmoil, toxic emotions, and the effects of stressful situations play a critical role in causing and exacerbating IBS and other lower-tract problems.

But the fact that this relationship exists actually raises more questions than it answers. How is it possible that mere feelings—of which you may not even be consciously aware—can give rise to these very tangible and uncomfortable sensations in the body? It is indeed puzzling. Most physicians describe IBS as a "psychosomatic disease" and accompany this diagnosis with the unsettling information that, although it's not serious or life-threatening, IBS appears to be incurable. In other words, patients are told that they must learn to live with it.

To most people, "psychosomatic" means it's all in the head. If that's so, why does it hurt so much in the belly?

Answering such a question involves unraveling some of the ultimate mysteries of human physiology. It requires an understanding of the integrated nature of the human body—of how nature has sewn us together using threads of intelligence in infinite variety. On a less abstract level, it means identifying the relationships among neurochemicals located in the brain and throughout the physiology, which influence every one of our thoughts, feelings, and bodily functions.

Let's begin our investigation where the ancient Ayurvedic teachers started theirs, by asking the ultimate question about human health: Must we become sick and grow old at all?

Their answer was an emphatic *no!*

The ancient sages knew that if the forces inside us are kept in harmony and in balance with the surrounding environment, we can become immune to illness altogether. This is truly the state of perfect health. But how can we create it in the everyday world?

Perfect health is possible only through perfect balance. In order to prevent any disorder, the physiology must be balanced in its nature, and in order for any disorder to be treated, we must first correct the underlying imbalance that caused it. In this chapter we'll focus on restoring balance as a solution to the unsettling feelings and toxic emotions that can cause IBS or any other bowel disease, and we'll explore a number of approaches that can help establish harmony at the most fundamental level of life.

In the West, instead of focusing on health and physiological balance we've been preoccupied with disease and dying for many centuries. This says much more about our particular view of life than it does about life's essential nature. In truth, life is immensely flexible, and the forces that cause it to endure are at least as strong as those that cause it to decay.

If you plant a pine tree on a downtown lot in a polluted city, it may live for fifty years; if you plant it in the country, its life span may increase to two or three centuries; in another location, perhaps in the Rocky Mountains, it might survive more than a thousand years. Which life span, then, is natural for the pine? It depends entirely on the situation; some forces are always working to preserve the tree's life while others are opposing it. The tree's ultimate destiny—a long life or a short one—depends on the balance or imbalance among those forces.

What's true for trees is also true for animate creatures. If the caloric intake and body temperature of a laboratory mouse are carefully controlled, the mouse's life span can be extended two or even three times beyond what would otherwise be the case. Yet a second mouse, exposed to abnormal stress, will very likely die in just a few weeks. It's important to note that at the time of their respective deaths all the internal organs of both animals will have aged to the same degree. The worn-out heart, liver, and kidneys will be uniformly "old" even though the first mouse lived perhaps fifty times longer than the second.

As human beings, we can choose and control our environment, which gives our life span enormous variability. At the time of the Roman empire, adult life expectancy was about twenty-eight years, while many experts estimate that by the year 2000, life expectancy may rise to ninety years for a healthy American. This huge change demonstrates a great deal of societal progress as well as an impressive response to a more biologically hospitable environment.

The control center for this flexibility is located in the genetic material contained in every one of the 50 trillion cells that make up your physiology. Actually, to speak accurately about any individual's life span, we must refer to the many life spans that are always taking place inside a human body. Remember that a typical cell in the lining of your stomach lives only a few days, a typical skin cell only two weeks, a red blood cell perhaps two or three months ... while some cells in the heart and brain appear to last a lifetime without ever reproducing!

The amazing thing about these various life spans is that the very same genetic material—DNA—controls all of them, from the very shortest to the very longest. Somehow your DNA is able to create all kinds of specialized cells, each with its own function and life expectancy. Skin cells and brain cells, in other words, are genetically identical despite the fact that one lasts much longer than the other. You can't even tell which cell's life span will be long or short by examining the cells themselves: The neurons in your brain, which last a lifetime, are all but identical to the olfactory cells in your nose, yet olfactory cells are replaced every few weeks.

It appears that life is so flexible and dynamic that one may legitimately ask why we don't survive even longer and live entirely free of disease. The answer, according to Ayurveda, is that we could do just that if we would only learn how to handle and balance the various forces that are at work in and around us. In fact, this can be accomplished simply by tapping in to our basic impulses toward growth and health—toward the sense of balance inherent in every cell of our physiology. In the West, scientists now refer to the state of optimum balance as "homeostasis." Ayurveda identified the same balancing principle of nature thousands of years ago, but even today the relationship between health and physiological balance remains largely unknown to most people. As a result, all too often the forces acting against balance and health gain the upper hand, and the body has no choice but to give way to the ravages of disease.

If we could really learn to live in balance at every level of our physiology, then our inner growth would have no foreseeable limits. The key insight, which Ayurveda emphasizes, is that such growth is intended by nature to be automatic. It's programmed into our very cells. Experiencing it is only a question of following the silent river of intelligence to its source. Truly, this is the final secret of creating perfect health.

How is all this related to finding a practical mind/body approach for resolving physical problems such as IBS? The answer resides in a deep understanding of the principle of balance. In order to create balance, we must simultaneously focus both on the many localized elements of the body as well as on the organism as a whole. To clarify this point, just look at your hand. The palm is like the root of the physiology, which binds the organism together into a whole. The fingers represent the localized parts, but all of the parts join together at the root to constitute one holistic organism. Our bodies are exactly like this, comprised of an infinite variety of aspects, all bound together by the source of intelligence. Because the fingers of your hand are all joined to the palm, a sensation experienced by any one of them will influence the hand as a whole, but a more fundamental sensation would occur at the level of the palm itself, which is the "root" of the whole hand. The dual principles are actually very simple. We balance the whole body by balancing the parts—and we balance the parts by stabilizing the body at the most fundamental level.

Since balance is the key, here are some practical steps you can take to create this balance from the most basic levels of your existence.

Begin with a process known in Ayurveda as "self-referral." This simply means that you look inward, inside yourself, in order to influence your next behavior or action. In our society, self-referral is very uncommon. One generally encounters "object-referral" instead, in which an individual relies on external cues to determine behavior. To free ourselves from object referral and to structure self-referral activity, we must begin by placing our attention on our internal cues. These are literally messages and signals provided by your physiology to move you in the direction of creating perfect health.

Nature has really provided us only two types of signals—a sense of comfort and a sense of discomfort—and either of these can be physical, emotional, or psychological. When you are feeling perfect in every respect, your behavior is that of self-referral. It is directed toward honoring the internal cues provided by the physiology. This behavior will produce not only success on the material level but balance from the deepest level of being.

When you experience emotions such as fear, anxiety, unhappiness, or anger, try to understand that these cues are indications that you've come "out of yourself" and are behaving according to object referral. This should not be confused with the sudden adrenaline surge that has come to be known as the "fight-or-flight" response. Fight-or-flight, at least under certain dire circumstances, can serve a genuine survival imperative. Object-referral behavior, however, derives from frustration and misplaced emotional discomfort. Behavior of this sort will not only fail to be successful on the material level, it can also create damage anywhere and everywhere in the physiology.

Obviously, everyone experiences negative emotions on a regular basis, but much can be done to free you from the grip of these sensations and to return you to your true self. The first step is an awareness of the fact that every emotion includes both a thought and a physical sensation. Every emotion, no matter how weak or strong, has these two components because every impulse at the level of the mind has a simultaneous impulse in the physiology.

When you feel overwhelmed by any feeling, try turning your attention to the emotion's physical component. When you feel upset, pause for a moment and allow your attention to settle on the sensations occurring in your body. If you close your eyes for a few seconds, your mind will immediately be attracted to some particular area of the physiology, perhaps your stomach or your heart. Just allow the attention to remain on that area for perhaps half a minute. Gradually you'll discover that the physical sensation begins to moderate. When you open your eyes, you'll find that the emotional component has also diminished.

The most powerful approach for dealing with negative emotions is to structure a level of awareness that is self-referral at all times, so that the perfectly correct response becomes a spontaneous and automatic part of the mind/body system. Even if negative emotions arise because of stressful situations in your life, you can become like a silent witness to them, with a firm balance remaining deep inside.

Meditation is one of the best ways to accomplish this, as has been confirmed by contemporary studies in America as well as by the accumulated experience of many generations in other parts of the world. Meditation can take many forms. Some involve the use of mantras—that is, sounds that are repeated silently or aloud in order to bring the mind to a new state of awareness. These sounds are not words in the usual sense; they do not refer to anything in the physical world, for example, in the way that the word *dog* refers to a four-legged animal. But mantras can have a powerful spiritual impact. They resonate very deeply in the mind at a basic level where sound itself can have meaning that is separate from language. Mantras can best be described as primordial, meaning "foundation" or "original."

We give instruction in primordial sound meditation at the Center for Mind/Body Medicine in California, but it is by no means the only meditative form that can be of benefit. The Breathing Meditation technique introduced here is very simple but can be extremely effective in freeing both body and mind from the effects of negative emotions.

Breathing Meditation

1. Set aside some time when you're free from work or family responsibilities. Find a quiet place where you will not be disturbed.
2. Sit quietly on the floor or in a straight-backed chair. Close your eyes.

3. Begin by simply exhaling and inhaling as you normally do, but gradually focus your awareness on the process of your breathing. But don't try to control or influence it in any way. Just be aware of the coming and going of your breath.

4. If you notice your breath speeding up or slowing down— even stopping for a moment—simply observe this. Don't try to resist it or encourage it; rather, allow it to pass.

5. Similarly, if your attention wanders or you become distracted in any way, don't resist. Just allow your attention to gradually and naturally return to your breathing.

6. Continue the Breathing Meditation technique for fifteen minutes. Allow yourself another few minutes for withdrawal from the technique, still sitting with your eyes closed. Then open your eyes and resume your normal activities.

A certain level of commitment is required in order to gain the benefits of meditation, but the results will more than justify the time and self-discipline required. I urge you to practice Breathing Meditation for twenty or thirty minutes in the morning and in the evening. Morning meditation should take place before breakfast, although if you're very hungry it may be best to eat something in order to prevent distraction. Evening meditation should be performed after you've had a chance to wind down from work but before the evening meal. As you settle in to this routine, the experience of restful alertness that is the essence of meditation will begin to have positive effects on your stress level and on your general state of mind throughout the day; this in turn will alleviate many emotionally based gastrointestinal symptoms. Indeed, you will gain access to resources of self-referral that can be of enormous benefit in every area of your life.

There are several other factors you should be aware of in order to keep your emotions in balance. Ayurveda identifies a type of behavior that is destructive to self-referral living, and to the intestinal tract in particular. This can be described as "stressed activity hurriedly done." Unfortunately, those four words summarize the lives of too many individuals—moving from one thing to the next, completely object-referral, without even full awareness of living, much less enjoyment of it.

In a sense, your body is always "digesting" the environment in which you live, and this is accomplished through your senses. So, balancing the senses is an important aspect of creating balance for the whole physiology. Ayurvedic music therapy, called *gandhama veda,* can help achieve this. Gandhama veda uses melodic sequences of sound to create balance in the individual mind and body as well as in the surrounding environment. There's no doubt that sound has an extremely powerful effect on any physiology. Research has shown, for example, that plants grow better when exposed to beautiful music and don't grow as well when subjected to loud, jarring sounds. Listening to music before bed or during stressful moments during the day can help to reset the senses into the self-referral mode. Information on sources for gandhama veda recordings can be found at the back of this book.

Ayurveda also recommends utilizing the sense of smell to create balance. Each of the five senses is actually formed by a different vibration in the quantum mechanical body, and each of these vibrations, or "languages," has a particular effect on the doshas. The language of aromas is quite complex. The human nose can identify as many as ten thousand different odors, and olfactory cells located on the membranes inside the nose pass straight to the hypothalamus, which is located in the brain. These olfactory cells are actually nerves—the only ones in the whole body that are exposed to air—and they're protected only by their thin covering of mucus. They are also the only nerves that regenerate, replacing themselves about once every three weeks.

The fact that smells go straight to the hypothalamus is very significant, for this tiny area of the brain is responsible for regulating dozens of bodily functions, including temperature, thirst, blood-sugar levels, growth, sleeping, waking, emotions, and digestion. To smell anything is to send an immediate message to the hypothalamus, hence to the whole body.

Specific aromas can be used to balance the three doshas. Aromas such as basil, orange, and clove influence Vata; Pitta is balanced more by sweet, cool aromas like sandalwood, rose, mint, and cinnamon. Special blends of aromas can be designed to benefit individual needs. Again, information regarding sources of Ayurvedic materials is available at the end of this book.

There are many other factors in your daily life that you must consider in order to reduce stress and balance your emotions. Are you trying to juggle too many responsibilities? Are you working too many hours? Do you bring home the anxieties of your job at night? In order to relieve any of these stresses, you must begin paying attention to your internal cues. The goal is certainly worth achieving: not only years added to your life, but full enjoyment of those years in whatever way you choose to define it. Regardless of whether you truly want to work twelve hours a day, or would deeply appreciate more time with your family, or would simply like to go off by yourself for a period of time, the first step is to "know thyself." The reward is perfect health through perfect balance in every facet of your life.

7

BIOLOGICAL RHYTHMS:

RIDING NATURE'S WAVES

The continuity of the body and the universe is one of the most basic principles of Ayurveda. Each rhythm and cycle of nature is understood to have a corresponding cycle in the human physiology. Collectively, these cycles are referred to as our "biological rhythms." There is a beautiful Ayurvedic aphorism that describes this relationship:

> *As is the atom, so is the universe;*
> *as is the microcosm, so is the macrocosm;*
> *as is the human body, so is the cosmic body;*
> *as is the human mind, so is the cosmic mind.*

In order to correct any imbalance in the body, it's essential to realize that our internal biological rhythms are dependent on and must be in harmony with the "external" rhythms in nature. Actually, these internal and external rhythms are just two expressions of the same natural cycles.

Every day the sun rises, the sun sets, and billions of different things happen in between. Nature is so beautifully arranged that no matter how different these things are, they are part of a single unifying rhythm—although, speaking more precisely, there are really rhythms nestled inside one another, like wheels within wheels. Modern medicine has disclosed many of the obvious cycles in our body: the heart beating every three-quarters of a second, the lungs swelling to inhale air ten to fourteen times a minute. But many of the body's changes remain mysterious. Why does a person typically weigh more in the evening? Why are our hands hottest at around two in the morning? Why is it that certain medical treatments may be more beneficial if given at specific times of day?

Ayurveda's answer is that each of us has master cycles governed by the quantum mechanical body and that the body is constantly trying to synchronize its rhythms with those of nature. Every day we pass through the various cycles, and we feel their influence through alterations in the function of Vata, Pitta, and Kapha. Ayurveda defines three phases of cycles that take place from sunrise to sunset and then repeat themselves between sunset and sunrise. The approximate times are as follows:

- From 6:00 to 10:00 (A.M. or P.M.) an influence of Kapha is predominant in the environment.
- From 10:00 to 2:00 (A.M. or P.M.) an influence of Pitta is predominant.
- From 2:00 to 6:00 (A.M. or P.M.) Vata is predominant.

One of the most basic aspects of living in tune with nature is to know and respect these master cycles that support our physical existence. We are meant to ride nature's waves, not to fight against them. In fact, our bodies are already riding them, or at least doing the best they can in the face of our contrary habits.

In the wild, animals instinctively follow natural signals. But nature has given human beings a unique ability to choose the times and places of our actions. Whenever we make these choices, we are at the very same moment receiving signals from our quantum mechanical body, and these signals tell whether we are in harmony with the rhythms of nature. As we've discussed, these signals appear in only two forms: comfort or discomfort. When we experience any degree of discomfort in the intestinal tract, or anywhere else in the body, it's a sure sign that we are fighting against nature's waves rather than riding them.

I'm sure you can think of many different rhythms in nature. For our purposes here, the twenty-four-hour cycle of day and night is most important. This cycle has a corresponding rhythm in the body, which scientists call the "circadian rhythm." While the most obvious expression of the circadian rhythm is the sleep/wakeful cycle, many other neurological and endocrine functions follow a twenty-four-hour cycle as well, including temperature fluctuations, hormone and enzyme production, and electrolyte excretion. The processes of digestion and elimination are also part of this twenty-four-hour tempo.

Animals in the wild exhibit cycles of hunger and elimination that for the most part are consistent within a given species. These patterns repeat themselves day after day. Although humans eat at many different times and manifest wide variation in other natural functions as well, Ayurveda teaches that there are ideal times when these activities can be undertaken in a natural and beneficial way.

The chart at the end of this chapter sets forth an ideal Ayurvedic daily routine. Each aspect of the routine is designed to help synchronize your biological rhythms with the rhythms of nature. Throughout the balance of this chapter, we want to choose some of the most important points of that daily routine that can help put your entire physiology in harmony with nature, while at the same time strengthening digestion and eradicating intestinal problems.

The morning is a special time in Ayurveda. This is the time when nature sends out its most delicate messages; it's also the time when you are most sensitive to these signals. Your nervous system has been constructed so that the sight of the dawn, the feel of still air on your skin, the sounds of birds and animals awakening, all set the stage for your full and active participation in life during the coming day.

The best time for arising, therefore, is an important consideration. In reviewing the master cycles of the day, you'll notice that 6:00 A.M. is a pivotal point. This is the junction between the Vata and Kapha periods of the morning. It's the growing influence of Vata during the early morning hours, in fact, that causes the birds and other animals to begin to awaken, because Vata is an active dosha, providing alertness, energy, and preparation for activity. For this reason, Ayurveda recommends arising at or even before this pivotal time of 6:00 A.M. By doing so, the mind and body will be under maximum influence of Vata, so you'll awaken feeling light, lively, and energetic.

From 6:00 to 10:00 A.M., however, the qualities of Kapha begin to become more evident in the environment. Some qualities of Kapha are heaviness, dullness, and slowness. So if you sleep until the middle of the Kapha period—around 8:00 A.M.—your mind and body will be primarily under Kapha influence as you awaken. This is one of the reasons why many people wake up feeling dull and groggy, needing many hours and sometimes several cups of coffee before they feel alert enough to face the day. Yet, just by arising early, you can become more alert and feel more in harmony with nature.

There is another important benefit of arising while the influence of Vata is still strong. Remember that it's Vata which is primarily responsible for the functions involved in having a bowel movement. For this reason, Ayurveda says that the ideal time for a bowel movement is in the early morning, soon after arising, while the influence of Vata is still lively. It will be easier to create a habit of having a regular bowel movement at this time of day than it will at any other time. It will also be more in accord with the natural rhythms of the body.

Conventional medical wisdom states that having as few as

two bowel movements a week is still within normal range. According to Ayurveda, however, one should ideally have at least one bowel movement each day in order to eliminate waste products and toxins from the day before. If this is not currently your situation, there's no need to worry, for the body is tremendously flexible in its ability to tolerate variations from the ideal routine. But it's wise to begin structuring a routine that will encourage this natural habit.

Drinking a glass of warm water soon after rising can gently encourage a morning bowel movement. Warm water activates the gastrocolic reflex, which simply means stimulating the bowel by placing something warm in the stomach. After drinking warm water, allow yourself five minutes or more in the bathroom to determine if your body is ready. Just sit comfortably with your awareness settled and see what happens. If after a few minutes nothing does, don't worry, and definitely don't strain. With time, many people find that this practice creates a habit of regular morning elimination. Once you form this habit, it will be easy to keep it for the rest of your life. Even if you are regular in your bowel movements at another time of day, try this routine for a few weeks and see whether your body naturally begins to shift to it.

It's best not to read while sitting on the toilet. Without becoming too technical, this is because reading involves subdoshas of Vata that govern mental functions, which are also responsible for Vata's upward flow. Since the subdosha Apana is responsible for the downward flow, mixing these two activities will confuse the physiology and create strain on Apana.

After the bowel movement, Ayurveda recommends a sesame oil massage as part of the daily routine. Most people find this one of the most enjoyable activities of their day. Requiring only a few minutes, the morning massage works by soothing the body's two master systems, the central nervous system and the endocrine system. Perhaps it's for this reason that Cherak, one of the original authors of Ayurveda, lavished praise on the practice of daily oil massage known as *abhyanga*. Cherak taught that abhyanga rejuvenates the skin, tones the muscles, eliminates impurities, and promotes youthfulness.

Abhyanga is also a good technique for beginning the day in a relaxed manner, both physically and mentally, which Ayurveda considers extremely important. Remember that people who view the day as a race against time hardly have the ideal approach for achieving perfect balance.

Instructions for performing the daily massage are provided on pages 76–77. During the massage, I advise that you spend a few extra minutes gently massaging your abdomen with the warm oil. If you follow this with a warm bath, both you and your bowel will be much less irritable throughout the entire day.

You should take your heaviest meal at lunchtime; this is an extremely important Ayurvedic recommendation. Moreover, you should try to take lunch at approximately the same hour each day. The best time is in the middle of the Pitta period, about noon or 12:30 P.M. The reason for this is quite straightforward. Since every cycle in the body has a corresponding cycle in nature, this is also true of Pitta, which is primarily responsible for agni, the digestive fire. The presence of Pitta in the body corresponds to the influence of the sun in nature. That's why the midpoint of the Pitta cycle is around noon, when the sun is also at its peak. It's also at this time that the digestive fires are most prepared to process food. In most cultures in the world, lunch has traditionally been the main meal of the day. It's really only since nations have become industrialized, with people bending their basic biological routines around their work, that heavy dinners have become popular.

You can think of the sun as a kind of support for the processes of digestion. When the sun is high in the sky there will be greater

AYURVEDIC OIL MASSAGE

HOW TO DO AYURVEDIC OIL MASSAGE

1. Start with cold-pressed sesame oil, available from your health food store. Ideally, the oil should be cured (purified) before using. (Instructions for curing are given below.) The oil should be warmed each day before you use it. One easy way to do this is to keep the oil in a small plastic bottle with a flip-top lid. Warm the oil by placing the bottle in a sink or container filled with hot water for a few minutes.

2. Use the open part of your hand, rather than your fingertips, to massage your entire body. In general, use circular motions over rounded areas (joints, head) and straight strokes over straight areas (neck, long bones). Apply moderate pressure over most of your body and light pressure over your abdomen and heart.

3. Start with your head. Pour a small amount of oil on your hands and vigorously massage it into your scalp. With the flat part of your hands, use circular strokes to cover your whole head. Spend more time massaging your head than other parts of your body.

4. Next, massage your face and outer ears, remembering to apply a small amount of oil as you move from one part of your body to the next. Massage this area more gently.

5. Massage the front and back of your neck and the upper part of your spine. At this point you may want to cover the rest of your body with a thin layer of oil to give maximum time for the oil to soak in.

6. Vigorously massage your arms, using a circular motion on your shoulders and elbows and long, back-and-forth strokes on your upper arms and forearms.

7. Now massage your chest and stomach. Use a very gentle, circular motion over your heart and abdomen. You can start in the lower right part of your abdomen and move clockwise toward the lower left part, to gently massage your intestines.

8. Massage your back and spine. You may have trouble reaching your entire back. Just do the best you can.

9. Massage your legs vigorously, using circular motions over your hips, knees, and ankles. Use long, straight strokes over your thighs and calves.

10. Finally, massage the bottoms of your feet. As with your head, this important area of your body deserves more time. Use the palm of your hand to massage your soles vigorously.

11. Follow your oil massage with a warm bath or shower, using a mild soap.

HOW TO PREPARE SESAME OIL FOR AYURVEDIC OIL MASSAGE

Ayurveda recommends using unprocessed, cold-pressed sesame oil, which is available at health food stores. Before using the sesame oil, it's best to cure it by following these simple steps. Curing increases the oil's ability to penetrate the skin.

1. Heat the oil to about the boiling temperature of water (212°F). To know when the oil is hot enough, simply add a single drop of water to the oil before you heat it. When the water crackles or boils on top of the oil, you can remove it from the heat. Or just observe the oil as it heats. When it begins to move and circulate in the pan, remove it from the burner.

2. If you like, you can cure up to one quart of oil at a time. This should be enough for at least two weeks.

3. **Caution:** Because all oils are flammable, be sure to observe proper safety precautions. Use low rather than high heat, never leave the room while the oil is heating, and remove it promptly once the proper temperature is reached. Be sure to store it in a safe place when cooling, out of the reach of children.

assistance for the digestive processes in the body, because the sun's energy will be synchronized with the physiological influence of Pitta. But when the sun is rising in the morning and setting in the evening, digestive capacity is weakened, because there is less support from the environment for the Pitta in the body.

By eating your lunch between noon and 12:30 P.M., you can take in even large quantities of food and still digest it properly. This will preclude the need to take a large meal near bedtime, which would be more difficult to digest.

This one simple recommendation can make a dramatic difference in your metabolism and elimination. Because digestion is stronger in the middle of the day, food will be more efficiently converted into energy, and your body will ultimately be more comfortable during the later stages of digestion.

Lunch should be taken in a settled environment, and every effort should be made to ensure that it's wholesome, nutritious, balanced, and tasty. The meal should be freshly cooked and taken in accord with all the principles you are learning in this book. Of course, I realize that eating a substantial lunch may be difficult for people who must cope with demanding work schedules. A healthy lunch may not be as convenient as a quick sandwich followed eventually by a heavy dinner. But a little creativity in this area definitely provides immense benefits in resolving all intestinal complaints. If you think it's impossible to arrange a good lunch each day, do your best with it for a couple of weeks and then decide whether it's worth continuing. I'm confident you'll notice benefits that extend well beyond the digestive tract.

Ayurveda also has recommendations for breakfast and dinner.

In the morning, when the sun is rising, there is less support from the environment for digesting heavy foods. Therefore, breakfast is an optional meal and does not even need to be taken. In any case, breakfast should be a light meal, such as milk and cereal, or herbal tea and toast.

The most important principle is to avoid producing any discomfort in the body. Individuals who have stronger appetites, especially those who have Pitta constitutions, may require more food for breakfast than do the other types. Kapha types, on the other hand, may find that they can easily skip breakfast and still feel very comfortable waiting for lunch. If you are currently in the habit of eating a heavy breakfast, I recommend that you try switching to a lighter one, which will provide you with more appetite at lunchtime.

At dinnertime, as the sun is setting, there is less digestive power than in the middle of the day, but more is present than at breakfast. For this reason, dinner should be taken on a regular basis, but it should be lighter than the luncheon meal. If you've been taking a balanced and solid lunch, you just won't be very hungry at dinner. If you eat only a sandwich or a light salad for lunch, you'll still be hungry later, and a heavy dinner followed within a few hours by sleep will strain your digestive tract and produce ama.

Your food at dinner should not be heavy, so take meats and cheeses sparingly and in general eat less than at lunch. Some examples of dinners that you may find very satisfying, perhaps to your surprise, are hot soup and bread, hot cereals, and assorted vegetables.

A final important point about the daily routine concerns bedtime. A tired body is not alert to its inner needs and is consequently more vulnerable to stress and imbalance. You may have noticed that when you allow yourself to become fatigued, you're more likely to react by internalizing stress in the form of gastrointestinal symptoms. We've already recognized the importance of rising early in the morning as a way of feeling fresh and alert all day, and as an aid in establishing a regular morning-elimination pattern. It follows that if you start to get up earlier but continue to go to bed at the same time, you are likely to be tired all day.

Another pivotal junction in the twenty-four-hour cycle occurs at 10:00 P.M. This is the meeting point between the Kapha and Pitta periods of the evening. The influence of Kapha during these hours is very evident. In the evening, after we've completed our work and the sun is setting, it seems like the whole environment is quieter, as if all of nature is settling down. Most people instinctively feel like sitting back and relaxing. Of course, if you live in a large metropolitan area you may wonder where this natural silence may be as you look out on the frantic activity of an urban night. But this is not the influence of nature itself; rather, it is an aspect of our modern lifestyle, which often brings us into conflict with nature's intention.

Observing nature, we find deepening silence and calm throughout the environment as night falls. If we allow it in, this settling effect will be reflected in our bodies, which by the end of the Kapha period, at 9:00 or 10:00, will begin to prepare for sleep. Remember that the qualities of Kapha are heaviness, dullness, and slowness—ideal qualities for bringing rest.

If you don't go to bed by 10:00 P.M., the environmental influence of Pitta begins to grow. Remember that Pitta is an active dosha whose qualities are lightness, sharpness, and heat. Most people find that staying up until 10:30 or later brings a new rush of alertness, which can remain strong late into the night. But what has really happened? By removing sleep from synchrony with the rhythms of nature, the sleep we eventually do experience will be shallow and restless. For those with sleep problems, sleep will be more difficult to come by during these later hours. So Ayurveda recommends taking adequate rest and choosing the hours of sleep for maximum accord with nature. Bedtime should be as close to 10:00 P.M. as possible, and then it will be natural and effortless to arise earlier in the morning.

Bringing your biological rhythms into accord with nature is an important part of establishing overall balance in your general physiology, which will then be able to produce these same balancing effects in the gastrointestinal tract.

AYURVEDIC DAILY ROUTINE

According to Ayurveda, an ideal day naturally structures itself into four time periods, as indicated below.

6:00 A.M. TO NOON

- Wake up not long after 6:00 a.m. Gradually train yourself to do so without an alarm clock.
- Drink a glass of warm water to stimulate the GI system and to encourage a bowel movement.
- Urinate and have an unforced bowel movement.
- Brush your teeth, including your tongue if it is coated.
- Perform sesame oil massage.
- Perform breathing meditation.
- Bathe or shower using warm water, not hot or cold.
- Exercise (see chapter 8).
- Eat a light breakfast.
- Try to take a 30-minute midmorning walk.

NOON TO 6 P.M.

- Eat an early lunch; this should be the largest meal of the day; avoid rushing or eating at your desk.
- Take a few moments to sit quietly after eating, then walk for 5 to 15 minutes to aid digestion.
- Perform breathing meditation in late afternoon or early evening.

6:00 P.M. TO 10:30 P.M.

- Eat a moderate dinner.
- Sit quietly for a few moments after eating, then walk for 5 to 15 minutes to aid digestion.
- Engage in light, stress-free activities during the evening.
- Bedtime at least three hours after dinner, but not later than 10:00 p.m. Don't read, eat, or watch television in bed.

10:00 P.M. TO 6:00 A.M.

- Sleep.

8

UNDERSTANDING EXERCISE

From an Ayurvedic standpoint, many of today's exercise techniques are very far from ideal. To understand why, let's begin with the purpose of exercise in traditional Indian medicine. Cherak, the great Ayurvedic physician, wrote:

> By physical exercise one gets lightness, capacity to work, firmness, tolerance of difficulties, diminution of physical impurities, and strengthening of digestion and metabolism.

Cherak went on to say that exercise is suitable for everyone, but that too much can be as damaging as too little. Also, since the proper amount and type of exercise varies from person to person, any activity should be properly suited to the individual.

The most important principle of exercise is that it should enhance rather than diminish energy, strength, and vitality. No matter which program of activity you are following, you should feel lively, strong, and energetic both during the exercise and afterward. If you feel exhausted and strained at any point, something is wrong with your particular exercise routine.

Regarding exercise, the three common mistakes people make are these:

1. Performing too little exercise or none at all
2. Performing exercises that don't suit them
3. Overexercising

Exercise can have many benefits related to IBS. In addition to reducing stress, healthy activity has a massaging effect on the colon, which soothes intestinal problems. But excessive, extremely demanding exercise can increase Vata and actually make an irritable bowel worse. This is especially true for Vata and Pitta types. Pittas enjoy competition and may choose exercise that is highly competitive in nature. Ideally, exercise should provide relaxation for the Pitta type, who tends to be highly driven, rather than serve as one more opportunity to make intense demands on the body.

As you might expect, physical training is an important means of communicating with your doshas, but each of the body types responds differently to exercise. Kapha types, who tend to have more muscular physiques and greater stamina, need regular exercise in order to feel lively and energetic, and they tolerate more vigorous exercise than either the Vatas or Pittas. Vata types tend to have smaller builds and are best suited to milder activities. Pitta falls between Vata and Kapha.

If you are a two-dosha type, let your physique be your guide in determining which exercise is best for you. If you are a Kapha-Vata type, for example, and have the typical muscular, athletic Kapha physique, then the Kapha category of exercise should be most suitable. Another Kapha-Vata type, however, may have the more modest physical build of a Vata and will respond better to the recommendations for that dosha. Here are some exercises that are best suited to each of the body types:

> **Vata:** dance aerobics, walking, short hikes, light bicycling
> **Pitta:** skiing, walking or running, hiking, mountain climbing, swimming
> **Kapha:** running, walking, weight training, aerobics, rowing, dancing

You shouldn't feel restricted to the activities on the list above. The best criterion for judging any exercise is whether you enjoy it. Find the activity that makes you feel good.

Walking is an exercise that suits all three doshas, and it's an ideal part of your treatment program for intestinal problems. Vary the speed and intensity of your walking according to your individual needs. A Kapha type may find that quick, aerobic-type walking feels best, while the Vata type will prefer more of a continuous stroll. An ideal addition to your daily routine would be at least thirty minutes of walking in the morning. Within a week or two, you'll begin to notice the benefits.

Ayurveda offers some other specific guidelines regarding exercise: In general, utilize about 50 percent of your capacity. If you can swim twenty laps, do only ten; if you can bicycle twenty miles, bicycle half that. Your capacity represents the total amount of energy available at a given time, beyond which you're completely tired and can't go any farther. The purpose of exercise is not to drain all your energy but to produce more of it. For this reason, never work out to your full capacity; stop while you still feel energetic and comfortable both mentally and physically. Of course, the principle of utilizing 50 percent of your capacity does not ignore the benefits of physical conditioning. As time goes on and your total capacity grows, 50 percent of that capacity will also be increasing.

Ayurveda recommends regular daily exercise, preferably seven days a week. The reason many aerobics programs recommend only three or four days of exercise per week is that they demand all the available energy of the physiology. This makes a recuperation period of several days necessary. The Ayurvedic principle is not "no pain, no gain" but "no strain produces maximum gain."

Your breathing and perspiration are good indicators of your response to exercise. Heavy breathing and a great deal of perspiration mean you're straining your body. Perhaps with more conditioning this level of exercise will suit you, but for now it's better to cut back.

The best time of day to exercise is during the Kapha periods, especially between 6:00 and 10:00 A.M. This is when the structure of the physiology is strongest and most tolerant of activity. And remember always to exercise on an empty or nearly empty stomach.

So far we've been discussing conventional types of exercises with which most people in the West are familiar. Ayurveda, however, includes a broad range of exercise that comes to us from the yoga tradition. We refer to these exercises as "neuro-muscular integration," because they benefit not only the muscular, cardiovascular, and metabolic systems but also serve to integrate mind and body in order to create specific and predictable physiological effects.

How is it possible for physical exercise to integrate mind and body? To fully grasp this, you need to understand the Ayurvedic view of your physical self. Imagine that you're an architect designing a new skyscraper. As part of that design, there will be certain junction points that bear more of the stress or weight of the structure than other points. Proper design of these points will be crucial to ensuring the stability of the building. In the same way, your body has certain junction points that Ayurveda refers to as *marmas*. These are extremely vital areas. If they are damaged, they can cause excruciating pain or severe imbalance. But if well balanced and enlivened, they can support health and bliss.

Marmas are described in Ayurveda as the meeting places of consciousness and physiology. Because of this, influencing a marma automatically influences many other parts of the mind/body system which have arisen from that junction point.

There are 107 marmas. Of these, three are the most basic, serving as central switching points that connect together all of the others. These extremely vital marmas are called *mahamarmas,* or "great marmas." Their names are *shiramarma, hridayamarma,* and *bastimarma*—and they are located in the head, the heart, and the lower abdominal region, in that order. Shiramarma, the mahamarma located in the head, plays a critical role in all mental functions, especially those involving understanding and discrimination. Hridayamarma, located in the heart, is important for maintaining the balance of the emotions. The heart, according to Ayurveda, is not only an organ to maintain circulation. As the poets have told us for thousands of years, it's also the center of all of our most intimate feelings.

Our focus in this book, of course, is on the third mahamarma. Bastimarma is responsible for many of the body's basic physical processes, including the normal functioning of the gastrointestinal tract.

Many of the recommendations made earlier act principally through the marmas. For example, the benefits of abhyanga, the daily oil massage, are achieved through a gentle stimulation of all the marmas on the skin. The skin's contact with the sesame oil has an immediate effect on the entire nervous system and a powerful salutary effect on Vata, Pitta, and Kapha.

The exercises described at the end of this chapter are derived from the yoga tradition. They provide a gentle, balancing, stimulating effect on the marmas, an effect caused by the stretching motion inherent in the yoga postures, as well as by focusing attention on the junction points of your physiology. Because the marmas are the meeting places of consciousness and physiology, they respond to awareness as well as to physical activity.

While you're doing these exercises, be aware that the intention is to produce a gentle effect on the marmas, not to create any sort of strain. Never exert yourself to the point of discomfort. Also, because attention is important in enlivening the marmas influenced by a particular posture, you will get the best effects from doing these exercises in a quiet place and from allowing your awareness to be innocently drawn to the vital points on your body.

I recommend making these exercises a part of your regular routine. They require only fifteen or twenty minutes per day, and the postures I've chosen are simple ones—but they do have powerful benefits for gastrointestinal health.

THE YOGIC SEAL
Yoga Mudra

Sit in a comfortable, cross-legged position on the floor. Move your hands behind your back and take your right wrist in your left hand. Now bend slowly forward, as if to press your chest against the floor. If you can, touch the floor with your forehead and then with your chin. But don't force; just bend as far as you comfortably are able, and take care to breathe normally throughout the exercise. Try to time your breathing so that you exhale as you bend forward, and then inhale as you slowly come back up.

Repeat three to seven times, holding the forward position for ten seconds during each repetition. As you progress, try to reduce the number of repetitions while increasing the duration of the forward bend, to a maximum of two minutes.

This pose is quite easy and is excellent for toning the digestive organs and relieving constipation.

STOMACH LIFT
Uddhiyana Bandha

With your feet slightly more than shoulder width apart, bend forward and place your hands on your knees. Now contract your stomach muscles, drawing them in to form a hollow as you exhale, completely emptying your lungs. Do not inhale while maintaining the contraction of your stomach muscles, but be careful not to go beyond the point of discomfort. Then relax your muscles and inhale slowly.

Repeat this exercise three to seven times. Your stomach muscles should remain contracted for five to thirty seconds with each repetition.

This exercise benefits constipation and indigestion. If properly executed, it requires little effort and can be used by anyone.

PELVIC POSE
Vajrasana

Kneel with your knees together. Your legs, from the knees to the toes, should be in contact with the floor as you lean slightly forward. Now slowly sit back on your legs, until your weight is directly above your ankles. Place your palms on your knees and breathe normally. Hold this pose for thirty seconds, then relax, lean forward, and repeat the exercise.

This exercise helps relieve flatulence and other symptoms of IBS, and it strengthens the leg muscles. If performed soon after eating, it will aid digestion.

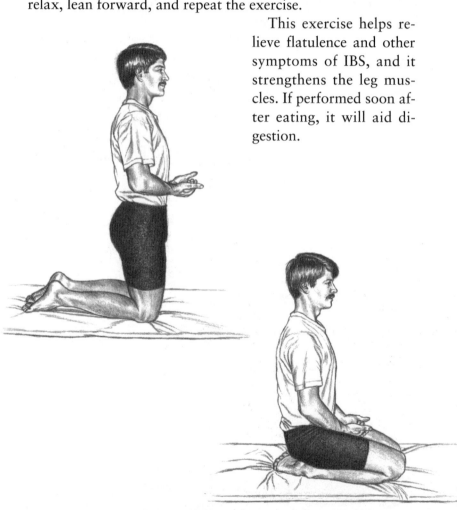

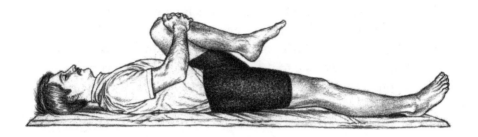

GAS-RELIEVING POSE
Pavanamuktasana

While lying flat on your back, raise your right leg and bend the knee. Inhale deeply through your nose. Hold your breath as you pull your knee against your abdomen, as if trying to kiss the knee. Do not strain or forcibly tighten the abdominal muscles. Hold this pose for as long as comfortable, then repeat with the left leg.

In addition to relieving gas, this exercise tones the abdominal muscles.

COBRA POSE
Bhujangasana

Lie face down with your forehead touching the floor. All your muscles should be completely relaxed. Now place your palms flat on the floor beneath your shoulders, keeping your elbows close to your body, as if to do a push-up. Slowly raise your chest and shoulders, while keeping your legs and the lower part of your body in contact with the floor. Look up and to each side of you, then slowly come back down. Breathing should be only through your nose. Hold the pose for ten seconds. Repeat three to six times.

This exercise relieves constipation and intestinal gas. There are also benefits for the back muscles and the spinal column.

9

CONSTIPATION, DIARRHEA,

AND INTESTINAL GAS

So far we've focused on Irritable Bowel Syndrome, but it's important to mention that several of its symptoms can also occur independently, even if full IBS is not present. In this chapter we'll look at three of these common problems—constipation, diarrhea, and gas—which at the very least are unpleasant, and which can sometimes be precursors of a more serious imbalance.

While we can discuss these conditions separately, please bear in mind that from an Ayurvedic standpoint they are all variations on a single theme. They all arise from disturbances in the various doshas and subdoshas that govern digestion and elimination. Different intensities and qualities of these disturbances will produce variations of symptoms, but many of the treatments will be the same.

CONSTIPATION

Constipation can occur for a number of reasons. Some of these are very simple, such as insufficient fluid intake or inadequate exercise. Long stays in bed are definitely bad for regular bowel habits, as are many widely prescribed antibiotics. Ask your doctor whether constipation should be anticipated as a side effect of any of your medications.

These last two causes of constipation are particularly widespread among elderly people, for whom the problem can become something of a preoccupation. Any physician who treats aging patients can attest to the high degree of attention many of them devote to their bowel movements. Although a certain degree of vigilance is appropriate to all our physiological functions, it is also true that "a watched pot never boils"—and there are certainly many other things to think about while waiting for nature to take its course. Let me mention once again the role medication plays in slowing the colon function of older people, many of whom take heart or high blood pressure medicines. These can cause constipation. If the medication can be changed or withdrawn, the situation will most likely improve.

For the majority of middle-aged or younger people, Western medicine considers constipation a dietary problem, arising from foods that lack "bulk" or "roughage." These terms refer to material such as dietary fiber, which is able to pass through the small intestine without being digested and is therefore able to provide the large intestine with a stool of sufficient size to be easily moved along by contractions of the colon's walls. If the stool lacks bulk, it enters the colon as a small, hard object that requires extreme contractions by the colon in order to pass through it. The patient experiences these contractions as painful cramps.

Ayurveda teaches that a healthy human being should have a regular daily bowel movement to eliminate waste products from the preceding day. For those with long-standing chronic constipation, it may require some time to achieve this goal even after adding more fiber to the diet and following the other recommendations in this book. Gradually, however, the body will readjust itself in order to correct imbalances. While this readjustment process is taking place, moderate constipation is usually not something you need to be overly concerned about. The human digestive system is tremendously flexible, and it can tolerate chronic constipation without showing any obvious damage. Indeed, Ayurveda believes that the presence of a stool in the large intestine has a positive, stabilizing influence on the body, because it prevents air from rising too high in the GI tract. Therefore, powerful treatments such as enemas or strong laxatives should be undertaken only with caution. They can result in side effects such as insomnia, heart palpitations, and anxiety, particularly the Vata mind/body type.

In most cases you should be able to resolve the problem of constipation simply by the gradual alterations of your diet we've discussed. But if you've tried this for some time and your constipation is still not completely resolved, there are a number of further suggestions that apply specifically to this problem.

According to Ayurveda, the underlying cause of constipation is a Vata imbalance. One of the characteristic qualities of Vata is dryness, and this often can contribute to the creation of small, hard, dry stools. To correct this, Ayurveda recommends making ghee a part of your daily diet. Ghee is the Sanskrit name for clarified butter, and at the end of this book you'll find information about how to prepare it at home. You can add ghee to foods at the table or use it as replacement for other oils when you are cooking.

Be sure to follow the morning routine of drinking warm water upon rising, followed by spending some time in the bathroom. This will help you to establish a regular bowel habit. If your constipation is severe in the morning, try taking a teaspoonful of almond oil shortly after you wake up. It is not necessary to continue this procedure indefinitely, but taking almond oil for one month will help begin to lubricate your bowel. You can also try eating a small handful of raisins at night before bed, which will stimulate normal elimination in the morning.

The best way to provide sufficient fiber in your diet is by eating freshly cooked vegetables, whole grains, and fresh fruits. However, the benefits of taking dietary fiber will not be felt immediately; it usually takes two or three weeks to see results. Ayurveda also mentions several specific foods for the treatment of constipation, such as grape juice, beets, split mung beans, and prunes or prune juice. Since everyone's system is unique, try experimenting to see which foods are most helpful to you in producing regular elimination.

A note of caution regarding fiber. Never ingest large amounts of commercially sold fiber supplements on the theory that "more is better." Unless fiber supplements are mixed with sufficient amounts of water, they form an inert mass that can actually make constipation worse. Be sure to drink at least several large glasses of water for every teaspoon of fiber supplement you ingest. Or, better, don't rely on supplements at all; instead, adjust your diet to include whole foods that are naturally rich in fiber.

As much as possible, stay away from laxatives. It's very easy to become dependent on them, which only creates more difficulty in establishing a routine of natural bowel movements. If, however, you are feeling very constipated and have not had a bowel movement for several days, an enema may be helpful. I recommend using sixteen to twenty-four ounces of body-temperature water. As with laxatives, frequent use of enemas is best avoided in order to establish natural bowel function.

DIARRHEA

Considered alone, diarrhea is a difficult symptom to interpret. It can indicate a serious bacterial infection or other gastrointestinal disorder, but much more often it originates from simple stress, a poorly prepared meal, or even from medications taken for other problems. Diarrhea can also develop when the moisture in food, for whatever reason, is insufficiently absorbed by the digestive system and by the small intestine in particular. This can be a serious condition. In some cases, the intestine may actually be secreting fluids as well.

Most of the time diarrhea is a self-limiting symptom; it goes away by itself. If you're struck by a sudden attack of diarrhea, and this is not something that often happens to you, avoid the temptation to take a commercially sold medicine. Instead, eat lightly or not at all for the rest of the day and lie down for a while in order to give your system more time to absorb moisture. Bear in mind that an acute episode of diarrhea is often your system's way of restoring equilibrium after excessive or unhealthy intake of food. If that's the case, there's certainly no benefit to suppressing diarrhea. Let it do its job. Once the attack has passed, make sure you drink more water than usual in order to overcome the dehydration that diarrhea brings on. Exasperating as it is, this dehydration can frequently cause an episode of constipation immediately after a diarrhea attack.

Dehydration brought on by diarrhea is often seen in very young children. Some researchers believe infant diarrhea is more common among bottle-fed breast-fed babies, but it can be brought on by a wide variety of infections and even by teething. Whatever the cause, in young children the problem should be taken seriously. An infant under six months of age who experiences diarrhea for even one full day should be seen by a physician, as intravenous replacement of fluids may be necessary. Although today this can easily be accomplished, a century ago dehydration brought on by diarrhea was the leading cause of infant death in the United States, and it still takes the lives of many children in other parts of the world.

If you have diarrhea that comes on suddenly and persists for more than a few days, you should consult a physician. And you should definitely do so if you've also experienced any rectal bleeding or weight loss.

If you have chronic diarrhea, and you've been evaluated by a physician without any specific medical cause being discovered, I believe the diagnosis of Irritable Bowel Syndrome should apply. If this is your situation, you can benefit by following all the recommendations provided in this book. But because loose stools can be a symptom of Pitta imbalance, I especially recommend the Pitta diet. Also, ingesting psyllium husks on a daily basis can help to tone the bowel. This is often useful in the treatment of both diarrhea and constipation.

INTESTINAL GAS

While everyone belches or passes gas from time to time, in some individuals gas can become a troublesome, uncomfortable, and embarrassing problem. Yet gas is normally present in the gastrointestinal tract. In fact, gas plays an important role in assisting the transit of matter through the intestine and colon.

Basically, gas in the GI tract derives from three sources:

1. Air swallowed from the atmosphere
2. Carbon dioxide formed in the first part of the small intestine as a result of a chemical interaction between acids produced in the stomach and bicarbonate formed in the pancreas
3. The action of the more than four hundred different bacterial species that normally live in the large bowel

Gas derived from the first of these categories is usually released in the form of a belch, while the second and third types account for what is politely termed flatulence. Let's consider the two problems separately.

Belching

Most people talk while they eat, and many people chew with their mouths open; both of these activities are inevitably accompanied by swallowed air. Belching soon follows, but not all belches are the same. For example, there is the spontaneous belch, which simply comes and goes. The belcher hardly gives a thought to his or her spontaneous belch, which often brings a feeling of mild relief, and in some countries is even considered a compliment to the cook!

However, there is also habitual belching. Here a preoccupation with belching has developed, often accompanied by a constant feeling of bloatedness that demands relief. However, in reality habitual belchers generally have no more air in their stomachs than do other people; they have simply made themselves more aware of air's presence as a way of manifesting anxiety. The best remedy to this situation clearly lies in lowering the stress level, but the physical sensation of bloating can also be diminished by reducing the amount of swallowed air. Just eat more slowly and with less conversation.

Last, but quite significant, everyone should be aware that an overwhelming urge to belch is frequently a symptom of heart attack. If the urge to belch is felt as a strong tightening sensation in the area of the diaphragm, which may be accompanied by pain in the arm or jaw, get help quickly.

Flatulence and Gas Pain

Sharp abdominal pain and persistent passing of wind are commonly perceived as symptoms of excessive intestinal gas. Yet, as with habitual belching, the real cause may lie elsewhere.

For example, people who suffer from "gas pain," which can be excruciating, often have no more gas in their systems than does anyone else—but their bowels may be irritated and as a result may be more sensitive to even a normal volume of gas. For these individuals, the problem of gas pain is very often an aspect of the larger problem of IBS.

This has been demonstrated by research studies in which balloons have been used to distend the colons of a group of IBS patients together with a control group. The IBS patients reported discomfort at a significantly lower level of balloon inflation than did the controls; what's more, the IBS patients experienced pain in a generalized, diffuse pattern that could include the entire abdomen and even the back. People with IBS just seem to be more sensitive to their "gut feelings," and to some degree this may account for the difficulties of treating the condition with conventional medications. Increased sensitivity may also cause IBS patients to experience the side effects of drugs more intensely than do other people. Consequently, they may be inclined to depart from prescribed dosages or even to discontinue medication entirely.

The problem of flatulence usually originates in the colon and is largely a function of what you eat. If your diet contains a great deal of protein, for instance, most of your digestion will take place in the small intestine; there will not be much left for the colon to do. But if you eat lots of carbohydrates, such as beans or nuts, sweets, or large amounts of meat, the task of digestion falls largely upon the many bacteria living in your large intestine. Moreover, these foods can alter the number and type of bacteria that are present. It is the action of these bacteria that produces gasses, several of which—hydrogen sulfide, for example—are foul-smelling. So if you and those around you are troubled by your flatulence, you can probably benefit from a reduction in carbohydrates, sweets, and possibly red meat if you have been eating it in large portions.

If you've been taking antibiotics, you should be aware that these can also bring on intestinal gas. Food allergies are another possibility. Chapter 10 discusses the problem of food allergies in greater detail.

Here are some further suggestions for dealing with intestinal gas:

1. In general, follow a Vata-pacifying diet.
2. When gas is a problem, it's especially important that meals be taken in a settled environment. Too much hurry, activity, or excited conversation will result in more swallowed air and, ultimately, more gas. Try not to speak while you are chewing or swallowing, and be sure not to eat too fast. Thoroughly chewing your food allows more saliva to accompany it to the stomach, and the saliva triggers the production of other digestive substances.
3. Avoid eating combinations of food that are likely to cause intestinal gas. Also avoid breakfasts that include citrus with starch—fresh orange juice and toast is a good example. These two food categories make contradictory demands upon your GI system and are almost certain to reach your colon in undigested form, with a predictably flatulent result.
4. Lassi, the beverage made from yogurt that was mentioned earlier, should be taken once or twice each day to help eliminate gas from the system.
5. A cup of ginger tea with honey can be taken five or ten minutes before every lunch and dinner. Aside from this, it's a good idea to drink as little as you can with your meal (especially avoid milk); if possible, try to drink nothing at all. This is because liquids dilute and weaken the GI tract's digestive substances.
6. End your meal by thoroughly chewing and swallowing about a quarter of a teaspoon of fennel seeds, which are very helpful in eliminating gas.

7. Last, be sure to take a few minutes of rest after each meal, before returning to your regular activities.

For controlling any or all of the symptoms discussed in this chapter, I recommend seeing a physician who has taken special training in Ayurveda. Often there are specific recommendations that can be made only after an individual examination.

10

OTHER GASTROINTESTINAL

PROBLEMS

ULCERS

Ulcer medications such as Tagamet, Zantac, and Pepcid are among the most widely prescribed drugs in the United States. Pharmaceutical companies have worked overtime to develop them, and they are indeed effective for many people. Of course, it would be better never to have developed an ulcer in the first place, but since the precipitating causes are not always easy to isolate, prevention can be difficult.

Two types of ulcers commonly occur: gastric ulcers, which are inflammations of the mucus lining of the stomach that have developed into open sores; and duodenal ulcers, similar inflammations in the uppermost portion of the small intestine, known as the duodenum.

Duodenal ulcers are generally the less dangerous variety. Furthermore, their incidence in the United States has been declining for several decades, perhaps because of changes in dietary habits. Most duodenal ulcers heal within a few months, but once you've had one it's almost certain to reappear. Stomach

acid is clearly a factor in causing duodenal ulcers, since people
who don't produce it don't get them. But an excess of stomach
acid doesn't mean an ulcer will necessarily appear. The critical
variable seems to be the ability of the duodenum to sustain the
presence of stomach acid in any amount at all.

Gastric ulcers, which occur in the stomach itself, are different in several important respects. They are less common, the
patient is typically older, and their incidence has not declined
in recent years. In general, gastric ulcer is the more serious of
the two varieties. The cause is again tied to stomach acid,
though too much of it is not necessarily the problem, since many
gastric ulcer patients actually produce less acid than the population as a whole. The stomach's inability to cope with its own
secretions seems basic to this condition.

For many years, stress has been considered an important
ulcer-producing factor. Acute stress can produce the "fight-or-
flight" response, one aspect of which is a shutting down of the
digestive processes. When this happens, acidic secretions as well
as undigested food can remain in the stomach for dangerously
long periods of time, and inflammation can result. It's interesting to note that ulcer surgery, particularly for the duodenal variety, often includes deliberate severing of the vagus nerve,
whose functions include transmission of the fight-or-flight response from the brain to the stomach.

In many cases Ayurveda diagnoses ulcers as a Pitta problem,
related to heat in several possible manifestations. These can include emotional heat in the form of anger or stress, biological
heat in the form of excess or poorly processed stomach acid, or
even dietary heat derived from heavily spiced foods. But even
if there is no imbalance of heat in any form, ulcers can still develop from a Kapha-based condition in which the mucus secretions of the stomach are insufficient to protect the tissue.

Ayurvedic treatment recommends a bland diet to promote
easy digestion. Irritants such as caffeine, alcohol, and tobacco
should definitely be avoided. Despite the fact that many ulcers

are associated with Pitta imbalance, and consequently with heat, cold or raw foods should not be taken. Do not skip any meals. Eat on a regular schedule in order to keep food in your system and prevent the direct exposure of tissues to acidic secretions. And always do your best to avoid conflict or worry during mealtimes.

INFLAMMATORY BOWEL DISEASE

Inflammatory Bowel Disease sounds similar to Irritable Bowel Syndrome, which we've been discussing throughout this book. This similarity can be deceptive. IBD is a separate category of more serious gastrointestinal disorders, including ulcerative colitis and Crohn's disease, which to some extent can be considered together. Although the clinical diagnosis and treatment of Inflammatory Bowel Disease is beyond our scope here, it is important to devote some space to these conditions. They affect the lives of a great many people, particularly in the United States and Europe.

Despite much research, Western medicine has not come to a firm conclusion regarding the causes of Inflammatory Bowel Disease. There seems to be a combination of genetic and environmental factors: The conditions often reappear among succeeding generations of certain families—especially, though not exclusively, among Jewish families—and they almost never occur among indigenous peoples in parts of the world where a high fiber diet is still the norm. As the numbers of such people diminish, however, the incidence of Inflammatory Bowel Disease has grown. Obviously, this suggests that diet is an important factor. The highly refined, low fiber foods common in the West can leave deposits of undigested material on the lining of the bowel, particularly of the large intestine. Just as a wood splinter can lead to an infection on the surface of the skin, residues adhering to the delicate gastrointestinal membranes can give rise to the ulceration, bleeding, and other symptoms of Inflammatory Bowel Disease.

Without going into great detail, the distinction between the two forms of IBD rests on the fact that ulcerative colitis generally begins in the rectum, with bleeding as the most frequent symptom. The primary condition does not extend beyond the surface of the colon, though in severe cases that entire surface may be involved. Depending upon the point of origin and the extent to which the disease has spread, people with ulcerative colitis may tolerate it for long periods of time without consulting a doctor, or they may become very ill quickly, with diarrhea and severe pain.

Crohn's disease involves the whole wall of the bowel rather than just the surface. In other words, the ulcers in Crohn's disease are deeper. It often appears first as pain in the lower right side of the abdomen, and it is frequently mistaken for appendicitis. Diarrhea can occur, as in ulcerative colitis, but this is usually not accompanied by bleeding. When bleeding is present, it can be alarmingly severe owing to the depth of the inflammation. This can penetrate through the colon into other organs and even the surface of the skin.

Both ulcerative colitis and Crohn's disease can be severely debilitating and even life threatening. Conventional treatment includes powerful drugs as well as surgery, which can include removal of affected organs.

Ayurveda's understanding of IBD is characteristically insightful. It relates the problem to the *chakras,* or concentrations of energy that control every aspect of our being. Unlike our physical organs, chakras do not exist as tangible objects within our flesh-and-blood bodies; rather, they are part of the subtle body, which exists on a separate plane and is connected to the physical body at several psychic junction points. There are seven chakras, with the first situated at the base of the spine and the seventh located at a point about four inches above the top of the head.

Ayurveda finds the origin of IBD in the first of these focal points, which is known as Muladhara, the "root" chakra. It is located at the base of the spine. This chakra is associated with the earth; it governs our ability to feel secure and "grounded" and to resist emotional disharmony. When problems such as Crohn's disease or ulcerative colitis appear, they indicate a weakening of support at the point of the first chakra. In other words, IBD derives from the presence of fear at a very basic level, and Ayurveda teaches that any successful treatment must take this into account. Once this fundamental problem is addressed, real growth and healing become possible both physically and emotionally.

Once the most severe symptoms of IBD have been brought under control, Ayurveda prescribes the herb asafoetida as particularly effective for maintaining colonic health. Asafoetida cleanses undigested food from the system and thereby eliminates ama. It is particularly useful in breaking up toxic accumulations that have resulted from excessive consumption of red meat or junk foods.

DIVERTICULOSIS

Diverticula are a form of hernia. They are outcroppings, like little pouches, that develop along the wall of the large intestine. They're like balloons that occur at the weak points of a bicycle tire. "Diverticulosis" refers simply to the presence of these pouches; when they become inflamed or infected, the condition is known as "diverticulitis."

Like many of the gastrointestinal conditions we've discussed, diverticulosis is more common in the West than in the less industrialized areas of the world. In fact, the condition was almost unknown in America until the introduction of refined flour and sugar late in the nineteenth century. As diet in the United States became more and more denatured, diverticulosis became increasingly common. Today it is estimated that more than half of all Americans have experienced this condition to some extent.

A high fiber diet throughout your life is the best way to prevent diverticula from forming. The fiber gives more bulk to your stool and prevents your colon from having to squeeze down extremely hard in order to move the stool forward. A straining colon is much more likely to develop diverticula than one whose job has been made easier by a high fiber diet.

Once diverticula have formed, they don't go away. But fiber can still minimize the chances of their becoming inflamed or possibly rupturing. When they do become inflamed (diverticulitis), it's often because a tiny piece of undigested food becomes lodged inside them—a condition often revealed by sudden rectal bleeding. In many cases surgery is necessary to correct the problem. The much easier course is to keep a healthy volume of fiber in your diet and to avoid highly refined, constipating foods.

APPENDICITIS

The appendix resembles a diverticulum at the lower right end of the colon. Diet has nothing to do with its presence, however; everyone is born with an appendix.

Although the appendix performs useful digestive functions in other animals, its presence in the contemporary human anatomy is difficult to justify. Like diverticula elsewhere in the colonic wall, the appendix is vulnerable to clogging by bits of fecal matter. And since the appendix can be almost a foot long, it can even develop a kink. The infection that results is known as "appendicitis," and if not treated the inflamed appendix can rupture, spilling bacteria into the abdominal cavity.

Appendicitis usually occurs in children and young adults up

to the age of 30. It often begins with moderate pain around the navel, which gradually moves to the lower right abdomen while at the same time becoming more severe. There may be fever, but not necessarily.

If you suspect you have appendicitis, it's important to consult a doctor immediately.

HEMORRHOIDS

Once again, here is a common GI tract problem that can usually be prevented by maintaining adequate fiber in the diet. If bulk is lacking in the stool, the resulting strain when having a bowel movement can cause enlargement of veins in the rectum or at the anus. If the affected vein is higher up in the rectum, where no nerve endings exist, there will be no pain, but bright red blood may appear on your toilet paper or on your stool. If the vein is lower down, pain can definitely be felt and bleeding may also accompany it. A clot may form in the broken vein, exacerbating the pain and irritating the surrounding anal tissue. Eventually these clots disappear by themselves, but meanwhile your discomfort may be considerable.

Hemorrhoids are easier to avoid than to cure. In addition to unhealthy diet, nervous temperaments seem more vulnerable to hemorrhoids, and many people report their onset at periods of stress or intense worry. Since they can also be brought on by poor posture and a sedentary lifestyle, exercise is important ... but not too much, since heavy lifting or the strain of extremely arduous running or climbing can also cause hemorrhoids.

Western medicine prescribes commercially sold ointments, hot baths, and sometimes surgery for hemorrhoids. Unfortunately, even an operation cannot guarantee that the problem won't reappear. There are many, many veins in the anal area, and every one of them is a potential hemorrhoid. Ayurvedic

treatments include externally applied washes made from astringent herbs such as haritaki and alum and from pomegranate, along with an avoidance of alcohol and spicy food.

If you feel a painful lump in your anus after a bowel movement, you almost certainly have a hemorrhoid. But if you experience rectal bleeding, do not attempt to diagnose yourself. You
should see a doctor regardless of whether swelling is present.

FOOD ALLERGIES

An allergy is a specific reaction produced by your body after
exposure to a certain substance. More precisely, it is a misdi-
rected response by your immune system. A distinction should
be made between a food allergy and a food intolerance. The
symptoms of these two categories may be similar, but a food
intolerance does not include an immune system response; therefore, it usually appears more slowly. An intolerance to clam
sauce, for instance, may occur an hour after eating or perhaps
not until the next day. But a true allergy usually presents itself
strongly and immediately.

When a food allergy is present, your body mobilizes to reject the designated food in the same way it would reject dangerous bacteria. Your cells produce defensive toxins intended
to neutralize the invader; these toxins also give rise to the sneez-
ing, swelling, and itching that characterize allergies. If you are
allergic to nuts, your immune system ferociously attacks any
nuts you have eaten. Since the nuts are just inert material,
they're unaffected, but you still experience the side effects of
your body's defensive reactions.

Why does one person's immune system mobilize against nuts
while another person's does not? There is no clear answer to
this. There does seem to be a relationship between allergic reactions and stress. An individual may show an allergic response
to a food or other substance for a number of years, after which

the allergy can disappear for an equally long period of time. Then it may suddenly reappear, usually when some other form of stress is present, such as difficulty in a job or a relationship. This stress puts the immune system in a state of heightened or even hyper-alertness, and the system produces an allergic reaction. Here the immune system is reacting like an overly sensitive mousetrap, which mistakes the slamming of a door for the presence of a mouse.

Milk, wheat, and eggs are common precipitators of allergic reactions. Ayurveda has identified other substances that cause allergies in specific doshas. Beans and corn, for instance, bring on reactions in Vata types; tomatoes, peaches, and strawberries do so for Pittas; and dairy products for Kapha types. If these foods are introduced into the system too early in life (which is frequently true of wheat or eggs), or if their introduction takes place in an atmosphere of anger or fear, the immune system can be incorrectly programmed, and an allergy may result. There are several remedies for this, the most obvious of which is to stay away permanently from the food in question. This will work, but it's really avoiding the problem rather than solving it. There are allergy shots, which work by desensitizing the immune system to certain stimuli, such as bee stings, but these are not effective for food allergies. I believe the best course includes temporarily withdrawing the problematic food while at the same time pacifying the immune system with such herbs as nutmeg, cardamom, fennel, cumin, and ginger.

These herbs will not weaken the body's defenses against genuine bacterial threats, but they will moderate the hair-trigger immune responses that are the basis of allergic reactions. The herbs will also have a generally calming effect on the emotions, which will be reflected in the mind/body system as a whole.

In Closing

The most important aspect of digestion is its absolutely central role in physical and emotional well-being. You are not only what you eat, as has often been pointed out, you are what happens to what you eat while it's inside your body. If what happens causes you pain or discomfort, your entire experience of living is diminished.

Food and the act of eating should be genuinely enjoyable. This is extremely important to health; it's very likely the most important of all diet-related issues. But don't let yourself be fooled about the true nature of enjoyment. The feeling that comes from daily overindulgence in sweet or greasy foods may become a habit, perhaps even an addiction, but it isn't really enjoyable—and anyone who has developed these food dependencies will surely attest to this if they're honest with themselves. For one thing, eating in this way no longer includes an element of choice; you simply know that you're going to eat fast food or candy today because it's what you ate yesterday and it's what you're going to eat tomorrow. This is not what I mean by enjoying food.

In order to take real pleasure in eating, and to give yourself all the benefits of gastrointestinal health, you must assume genuine control. Once you begin choosing a variety of foods—ideally, all six Ayurvedic tastes should be represented—you'll begin to notice positive changes in every area of your life, and you'll continue to develop a healthier diet. You'll do this easily and naturally, without straining. Indeed, strain itself is a major adversary of gastrointestinal health: Straining to eat a great deal of certain foods, straining to stay away from others, strain on the part of the digestive organs, even strained bowel movements are all symptoms of digestive imbalance. By discovering the real areas of strain in your diet—and in your life—and by making meaningful changes to eliminate them, you can achieve perfect health.

There's no reason you should settle for anything less.

RECIPES

HOW TO PREPARE GHEE

Ghee is clarified butter, which means that the butter has been purified. It is a very refined food and is considered highly energizing. Ghee can be used instead of butter on toast and other foods. It is also ideal as a cooking oil, because, unlike butter, it does not burn. Ghee can be purchased in many groceries and health food stores, or you can make it yourself:

1. Place one or more pounds of unsalted butter in a deep stainless steel pan on medium-low heat. Watch carefully to be sure that the butter doesn't scorch while melting.
2. As the butter heats, its water content will begin to boil away. After thirty to forty minutes, milk solids will appear on the surface of the liquid and also at the bottom of the pan.
3. Be alert to remove the liquid ghee from the heat as the milk solids turn golden brown at the bottom of the pan. You

may notice tiny bubbles rising from the bottom of the pan. Be careful that the ghee doesn't burn.

4. While the ghee is still hot, pour it through a stainless steel strainer that has been covered with a cotton cloth. Use a stainless steel or glass bowl to catch the ghee as it pours through the strainer. Be careful not to splash any of the hot liquid on your hands. It is not necessary to refrigerate ghee, but you may do so if you prefer.

HOW TO PREPARE LASSI

To make four servings, place ¼ teaspoon of cardamom, a pinch of saffron threads, and three tablespoons of hot water in a blender. Blend for ten seconds. Now add two cups of plain yogurt, two cups of cool water, and two tablespoons of sugar; blend until smooth. Lassi should be refrigerated until use.

BIBLIOGRAPHY

Frawley, Dr. David, and Dr. Vasant Lad. *The Yoga of Herbs.* Twin Lakes, Wisconsin: Lotus Press. 1986.

Janowitz, Henry D., M.D. *Your Gut Feelings.* New York: Oxford University Press. 1987.

Kapoor, L. D. *Handbook of Ayurvedic Medicinal Plants.* Boca Raton, Florida: CRC Press, Inc. 1990.

Oppenheim, Michael, M.D. *The Complete Book of Better Digestion.* Emmaus, Pennsylvania: Rodale Press. 1990.

Peiken, Steven R., M.D. *Gastrointestinal Health.* New York: HarperCollins. 1991.

SOURCES

More information on mind/body and Ayurvedic treatments, products, herbs, and educational programs can be obtained from the following organizations.

Quantum Publications
P.O. Box 1088
Sudbury, MA 01776
800-858-1808

Sharp Institute for Human Potential and Mind/Body Medicine
7630 Fay Street
La Jolla, CA 92038
800-82-SHARP

Ayurvedic Institute
1311 Menaul N.E., Suite A
Albuquerque, NM 87112
505-291-9698

American Institute of Vedic Studies
P.O. Box 8357
Santa Fe, NM 87504

American School of Ayurvedic Sciences
10025 NE 4th Street
Bellevue, WA 98004
206-453-8022

Maharishi Ayurved Products
P.O. Box 541
Lancaster, MA 01523
800-255-8332

INDEX

About the Author

Deepak Chopra, M.D., is Executive Director of the Sharp Institute for Human Potential and Mind/Body Medicine in La Jolla, California. The institute offers mind/body and Ayurvedic therapies in outpatient and residential settings in association with the Center for Mind/Body Medicine; training in mind/body and Ayurvedic medicine for health professionals and the general public; and research to validate the effectiveness of mind/body treatments. For further information, please call 1-800-82-SHARP.